The Transformative Let Them Power of Letting Go Theory for Control Less and Live More Book

Unlock Your Potential by Releasing What You Can't Control

"The Transformative Let Them Power of Letting Go Theory for Control Less and Live More Book"

Library of Congress Cataloging-in-Publication Data

Available upon request.

Contact Email: mspublishing2003@gmail.com

Cover Design by HS Publishers

Printed in USA

Table of Contents

Introduction: The Power of Two Simple Words

The Life-Changing Shift You've Been Waiting For

What if the secret to your happiness, success, and love was never something complex or unattainable? What if, instead, the key to it all could be found in two simple words?

Let them.

It sounds deceptively simple, doesn't it? But these two words, "Let them," can completely revolutionize the way you live your life. They hold the potential to free you from the pressure, anxiety, and struggle that come from trying to control everything and everyone around you. You don't have to keep carrying the weight of the world on your shoulders. You don't have to micromanage your relationships, your career, or your future. Instead, you can shift your focus to what truly matters—**your own well-being, happiness, and growth.**

If you're anything like I used to be, you've likely spent far too much time trying to control things that are beyond your reach. You've tried to manage how people perceive you, how they act, what they say, and perhaps even how they feel. You've bent over backward to appease others—whether it's family, friends, colleagues, or strangers—and in the process, you've neglected

yourself. You've sacrificed your own happiness, desires, and peace of mind in the name of control.

That was my story. For years, I lived in a constant state of stress, frustration, and exhaustion because I was trying to control everything. I tried to manage people's expectations, please everyone around me, and keep all the balls in the air. But no matter how hard I tried, I never felt fulfilled. I felt drained. I felt stuck.

But then, everything changed.

The moment I discovered the simple but profound power of **"Let them"**, my world began to shift. I learned that the secret to living a life filled with joy, clarity, and peace wasn't about trying to control every external factor. Instead, it was about **letting go**—letting go of the need to control what was never mine to control.

In this book, I'll teach you how to apply these two words to every area of your life—relationships, work, self-image, and more. But first, I want to share how this powerful mindset came into my life and how it can change yours, too.

My Personal Story: A Journey from Control to Freedom

I've always been someone who prided myself on being a "doer." I thrived on setting goals, ticking off to-do lists, and, quite honestly, on being perceived as someone who had everything together. I thought that to succeed—whether in my career, relationships, or personal life—I had to manage it all. The problem was, the more I tried to control, the more my life felt out of control.

I can still vividly remember the moment I realized I was suffocating myself with the weight of all this control. It was during a particularly overwhelming period in my career. I had a demanding job, a busy social life, and a growing list of responsibilities that seemed endless. I was constantly juggling commitments, trying to meet everyone's expectations, and pouring energy into fixing problems that weren't mine to fix. The result? Stress. Anxiety. A constant feeling of burnout.

I wasn't just tired—I was emotionally exhausted. I was giving and giving and giving, but in return, I felt empty. I had lost sight of what truly mattered: **me.** I'd spent so much time trying to manage how others saw me, how they thought about me, and how they felt about me that I had neglected my own needs and desires.

And then, one day, I hit a wall.

I was sitting in my office, staring blankly at my computer screen, feeling the weight of everything pressing down on me. In that moment, a thought crossed my mind that would change everything:

What if I didn't have to control all of this? What if I could just... let them be?

I wasn't sure what that meant at first, but I knew in that instant that I had to stop trying to manage things beyond my control. I needed to stop worrying about what other people thought. I needed to stop chasing approval. I needed to stop carrying the emotional weight of everyone's expectations.

So, I decided to give it a try.

I started small. I let go of my constant need to check in on everyone else's opinions and behaviors. I set clearer boundaries with people who were draining my energy. I stopped micromanaging at work and allowed my team to do their jobs without feeling like I had to oversee every little detail. I even let go of my need to always be the perfect friend, daughter, and partner.

And slowly, my life began to change.

I felt lighter. More focused. I was finally able to connect with what I truly wanted and needed in my life, and for the first time in years, I felt like I was living authentically. I wasn't trying to please anyone else or be someone I wasn't. I was simply *being*—and that was enough.

It was in this moment of surrender that I realized: **Letting them be, and letting myself be, was the key to everything I had been seeking.**

Why "Let Them" Is the Key to Unlocking Your Happiness, Success, and Love

It may seem counterintuitive at first. **Isn't control supposed to bring us peace and success?** Aren't we taught to take charge of our lives, be the captains of our own ships?

Yes, in many ways, we *are* the creators of our own reality, but the key to creating a peaceful, successful, and joyful life is realizing that there are **limits** to what we can control. We are not responsible for how others think, feel, or act. We cannot control the future, nor can we control the past. We can only control our responses, our actions, and our mindset in the present moment.

In essence, control is an illusion. And the more we hold on to that illusion, the more we suffer.

Letting go of the need to control everything around us isn't about giving up or becoming passive. It's about choosing to **focus on what truly matters—your own happiness, growth, and peace.** It's about trusting that the things you cannot control will unfold as they are meant to, and that you don't need to manage them in order to be successful or at peace.

This is where the power of **"Let them"** comes into play.

Letting others be who they are—without needing to change them or fix them—frees you from the weight of constantly trying to please, manage, or fix what isn't yours to fix. Letting go of your need to control how people perceive you opens the door to **authenticity**. Letting go of the need to be perfect allows you to embrace your **humanity**. Letting go of the constant pressure to meet external expectations helps you **prioritize your own needs**.

This is not to say that you should abandon responsibility or stop caring about people and things that matter to you. It's about recognizing the **boundaries** of what's in your control. You are responsible for your thoughts, your emotions, and your actions—but you are not responsible for managing others' behavior or controlling every outcome.

The famous **Mahatma Gandhi** once said:

"You must not lose faith in humanity. Humanity is an ocean; if a few drops of the ocean are dirty, the ocean does not become dirty."

This quote speaks directly to the heart of the **Let Them** philosophy. It reminds us that we can still love, care for, and engage with others without taking on their burdens, their flaws, or their expectations. You can be part of the ocean without needing to change every drop in it. You can engage with life in an authentic and powerful way, while also letting go of the need to control everything around you.

One of the most freeing things I learned during my own journey was that I don't have to fix everything, and I don't have to control every outcome. In fact, the more I let go, the more I saw things naturally falling into place. I found that when I stopped trying to force solutions, the right opportunities and people came to me, almost as if by magic. I allowed things to unfold without resistance, and that's when the real magic happened.

Success isn't about rigidly controlling every situation— it's about responding to life with trust and authenticity. Happiness isn't about managing every outcome—it's about embracing the present moment and finding peace within it. **Love** isn't about trying to control or change others—it's about loving them for exactly who they are, flaws and all, and giving yourself the same grace in return.

As you read through this book, I want you to remember this one thing:

You don't have to control everything. You just need to let things unfold naturally and focus on what you can control—yourself.

It's time to **Let Them.**

The Power of Letting Go: A Revolutionary Approach to Living

The concept of **Let Them** may sound simple, but it's one of the most powerful shifts you can make in your life. It's not about giving up; it's about stepping into your own power. It's not about ignoring what's important; it's about embracing what's within your control.

By the end of this book, you'll learn how to apply the **Let Them Theory** to every area of your life—from relationships to work to your inner peace. You'll learn how to let go of what doesn't serve you, how to stop worrying about what others think, and how to build a life that feels aligned with your true self. The journey you are about to take will help you reclaim your energy, your happiness, and your sense of self.

Are you ready to **Let Them**? Are you ready to reclaim your life and unlock the freedom you deserve?

Chapter 2: What Does "Let Them" Really Mean?

The Power of Surrender and Acceptance

When you first hear the words **"Let them,"** you might think it means giving up. Surrendering. Abandoning responsibility. But this isn't about giving up—it's about giving **yourself** freedom. It's about stepping back, not to relinquish your life to fate, but to stop wasting energy on trying to control everything around you. This chapter is about understanding that the power of "Let them" is not about surrendering to circumstances, but about **surrendering to your own peace** and recognizing that not everything is yours to control.

At first, this idea can feel uncomfortable. We've been taught our whole lives that control is a sign of strength. We think that to succeed in life, we must micromanage everything—from our careers to our relationships. But what if the truth was the opposite? What if the key to success, happiness, and fulfillment lay not in control, but in **letting go**?

Let me take you back to a personal story of mine, a moment when the concept of **"Let them"** truly clicked for me.

Personal Story: The Illusion of Control

A few years ago, I found myself in a relationship that I thought was everything I'd ever wanted. He was kind, intelligent, and successful. But despite all of the outwardly perfect qualities, something felt off. I couldn't put my finger on it, but there was a constant tension, a subtle undercurrent of dissatisfaction between us.

I kept thinking, *Maybe if I just worked a little harder, things would get better.* I began controlling the dynamic, subtly trying to influence his behavior—what he wore, how he communicated, what we did on weekends. I made small suggestions, "Hey, I think you'd look really good in that shirt" or "Maybe we should try this new thing this weekend?" The more I tried to *nudge* him into the ideal version of himself that I imagined, the more resistance I met. He pulled away, and I grew frustrated. It was as if everything I did to control the relationship was pushing him farther out of my reach.

I realized then that I had been holding onto the illusion that I could shape everything around me to fit my expectations. But what I was actually doing was suffocating the very relationship I cared about. I needed to **let him be** who he was—not who I wanted him to be. I needed to step back and accept him fully, without trying to control every aspect of our connection.

It was in that moment, with my heart heavy yet clear, that I finally understood the power of **"Let them"**—not just in relationships, but in life.

Surrender: Letting Go of What You Can't Control

When we talk about the power of **surrender**, it's important to understand that surrendering doesn't mean passive resignation. It doesn't mean giving up on your goals or dreams. It means **accepting** what is beyond your control, trusting that you are still capable of making choices within your sphere of influence.

Surrender is about **relinquishing the need to control outcomes**—and paradoxically, this is when you often experience the greatest success. The more we try to control things that are not within our power, the more we block the natural flow of life and opportunity.

Consider the words of **Eckhart Tolle**, the author of *The Power of Now*, who speaks so beautifully about the peace that comes with surrender:

"Surrender is the simple but profound wisdom of yielding to rather than opposing the flow of life."

When we resist the flow of life by trying to control things we can't, we create tension, stress, and frustration. But when we surrender to the natural course of events, we allow life to unfold as it should—without forcing, without resistance.

One of the most profound lessons I've learned in life is that surrender isn't about quitting; it's about acceptance. It's about saying, *I accept that some things are out of my hands* and choosing to focus on what **is** within my control—my thoughts, my reactions, and my choices.

Acceptance: The Foundation of Peace

Acceptance is the flip side of surrender. It's the practice of acknowledging reality as it is, without judgment or resistance. And here's the key—acceptance is not about condoning poor behavior or being passive in the face of challenges. It's about **recognizing** what is and then choosing how to respond to it.

The moment I accepted that I couldn't control my partner's actions or feelings, I felt a weight lift off my shoulders. Instead of being frustrated that he wasn't acting the way I wanted, I began to ask myself: *What do I need to change within myself to move forward with peace?*

In that moment, I chose to **accept** who he was, not who I wanted him to be. And with that acceptance, I was able to approach the relationship in a healthier way, releasing the constant pressure to control and instead, creating space for mutual respect, freedom, and love.

The great **Mahatma Gandhi** spoke about the importance of acceptance in our relationships and in the world:

"You must be the change you wish to see in the world."

Gandhi's words remind us that true change begins within ourselves. Instead of demanding that others change to fit our desires, we must first change our own perspectives, and that starts with acceptance.

Acceptance is not about approving of everything around us, but about **coming to peace with it**. When we stop fighting against what we cannot control, we free up energy to focus on what we can—and that's when transformation happens.

How Letting Go of Control Transforms Your Relationships

When we talk about **letting them**—whether it's letting go of control, judgment, or expectations—it's vital to understand how this applies to our relationships. The more we try to control the people in our lives—our partners, our friends, our colleagues—the more we risk pushing them away.

I'll never forget a conversation I had with a dear friend of mine who was struggling in her marriage. She was frustrated because her husband was, in her words, "not stepping up." He wasn't taking initiative in their relationship, in their home, or in their family life. She would constantly nag him about the things he should do, the ways he should behave, and the decisions she thought he should make.

I listened to her for a while, and then I asked, "Have you tried letting him be who he is, without the pressure of your expectations?"

She paused, clearly taken aback. "What do you mean?" she asked.

I explained that often, when we hold onto rigid expectations of others, we actually create a wall between us. We demand that people conform to our vision of who they should be, instead of accepting them for who they are in the present moment. And when we try to control them, we push them away—emotionally, mentally, and sometimes physically. Instead, I suggested, try letting go of the need to control his actions or behaviors. Try accepting him fully and see what happens.

A few months later, my friend called me with a transformation story. She had let go of her constant nagging and expectations, and as a result, her relationship with her husband had completely shifted. He started taking more initiative on his own, without her prodding. He began to feel **respected** and **valued** in a way he hadn't in years. Instead of feeling controlled, he felt trusted and free. The power of **letting him** be who he was created space for their relationship to flourish.

This is one of the most profound effects of **letting them**—whether it's your partner, your friends, or your coworkers. The moment we stop trying to control others, we create the space for them to **step into their own power**.

As **Deepak Chopra** wisely says:

"In the process of letting go, we make room for something better."

How Letting Go of Control Transforms Your Work Life

The idea of **letting go** in the workplace may seem counterintuitive. After all, most of us are conditioned to believe that success at work is about being in control—managing our time meticulously, controlling the flow of tasks, and maintaining authority. But what if the key to succeeding at work wasn't about controlling everything? What if it was about letting go of perfectionism and trusting in others to do their part?

I've had my own struggles in the workplace, especially earlier in my career when I was trying to climb the corporate ladder. I felt as though I had to prove myself by taking on everything—doing everyone else's work, micromanaging the details, and always being the one to step up. But this led to burnout and frustration. I couldn't keep up with the pace, and my relationships with colleagues were strained because I was trying to control everything.

When I began to **let go** of my need to micromanage and control every outcome, I found that I became more effective. I trusted my team to do their jobs without hovering over them. I allowed my colleagues to bring their own expertise into the process, and in doing so, we achieved greater results. I learned that **true leadership** isn't about controlling the people you work with; it's about empowering them, trusting them, and letting them use their own talents and strengths.

The famous leadership expert **John C. Maxwell** once said:

"Leadership is not about being in charge. It's about taking care of those in your charge."

In the workplace, this means **letting others be** who they are and trusting them to do their best work. When you release control, you empower those around you to step up, take ownership, and bring their full potential to the table.

Letting Go for a More Fulfilling Life

Ultimately, letting go of the need to control everything isn't just about improving your relationships or career—it's about finding inner peace and fulfillment in your life. When you accept what you can't change, you make room for **growth, joy, and success** in areas that truly matter.

By choosing to **let them be**—whether it's people, situations, or outcomes—you open yourself to the beauty of life as it unfolds, instead of forcing it into a shape you think it should take. You release the burden of control, and in return, you receive a life of more ease, flow, and fulfillment.

As **Wayne Dyer** said:

"You cannot always control what goes on outside. But you can always control what goes on inside."

This chapter is just the beginning of your journey toward understanding the true power of **letting go** and **letting them be.** By embracing surrender and acceptance, you can transform not only your relationships and work life but your entire experience of the world.

In the next chapter, we'll explore how to **practically apply** the "Let Them" philosophy in your everyday life and start creating the life you've always desired.

Chapter 3: Reclaiming Your Personal Power

The Psychology Behind Letting Go

When you begin the journey of **letting go**, you might feel liberated at first—but you may also experience discomfort. After all, giving up control goes against what many of us have been taught. We've been conditioned to believe that success and happiness come from exerting control over our circumstances, our relationships, and our environment. Yet, the true secret to reclaiming your personal power lies not in controlling everything around you, but in learning to let go of what isn't yours to control.

Letting go can be one of the most powerful tools for personal empowerment, but it requires a deep understanding of how our minds work. The psychological principle that underlies this process is **the illusion of control.**

We've all experienced moments when we believed that by managing every detail—by obsessing over every choice, every outcome, and every person's reaction—we could somehow create a perfect world. This illusion of control can be traced back to a psychological phenomenon known as **locus of control**.

The **locus of control** refers to the degree to which individuals believe they have control over the events in their lives. People with an **internal locus of control** believe that their own actions and decisions shape their destiny, whereas those with an **external locus of control** tend to believe that external forces, such as luck or other people, have a greater influence over their lives.

Here's the catch: When we operate from an **external locus of control**, we give away our personal power. We surrender our ability to create our own outcomes and become reactive instead of proactive. We become dependent on others, circumstances, or even random chance to dictate our happiness. This is when we start feeling **stuck** or frustrated because we're continuously trying to manipulate the uncontrollable, and we drain ourselves in the process.

One of the most profound realizations I had when I began my own journey of reclaiming my personal power was understanding that the only person I could control was **me**. I could not control my partner's actions, my boss's decisions, or even the outcomes of my hard work. But I could control my responses, my choices, and my focus. And that, in turn, became my greatest source of power.

As **Carl Jung**, one of the founding figures of modern psychology, famously said:

"I am not what happened to me, I am what I choose to become."

This quote is a reminder that our power is in our choices, not in our circumstances. The more we relinquish the need to control the uncontrollable, the more we reclaim our own power.

How to Stop Giving Away Your Energy and Focus

One of the most significant ways we give away our power is by allowing our energy and focus to be constantly pulled in directions that don't serve us. When we focus on things we can't control, we're essentially **depleting** our energy reserves. Whether it's obsessing over how others perceive us, worrying about things that may never happen, or trying to manage external outcomes, we divert our mental and emotional energy away from the things that **matter** most—our own growth, happiness, and sense of peace.

I remember a time in my life when I was deeply invested in trying to **please everyone**. I was always worried about what others thought of me—how I came across to my friends, my family, my colleagues. This constant preoccupation with seeking approval drained me. I found myself staying up late, overthinking conversations, re-playing past interactions, and constantly adjusting my actions to fit the expectations of others. I had essentially outsourced my peace to everyone around me.

The more I tried to control how others saw me, the more I lost sight of what mattered to me. My energy was spent on external validation, not on cultivating my own sense of self-worth. This is a prime example of how easily we give away our personal power. By investing so much mental energy in managing the perceptions of others, I was leaving little energy left to focus on my own desires and well-being.

Over time, I realized that I had to stop caring about what others thought—at least to the extent that it affected my peace of mind. I had to let go of the need for constant validation and trust that I was enough just as I was.

As **Wayne Dyer**, a renowned self-help author, put it:

"When you are at peace with yourself, the world around you will also be at peace."

It's easy to get caught up in worrying about others' opinions, but the truth is, their perceptions are often based on their own fears, insecurities, and experiences, not your true essence. When you let go of the need to control these perceptions, you make space for your own authenticity to shine through. The more authentic you become, the more energy you free up for your own personal growth and fulfillment.

To stop giving away your energy and focus, you must begin to identify where your attention is being diverted and take action to reclaim it. Ask yourself:

- Where are you investing your energy that isn't serving you?

- What are you focusing on that is outside your control?

- How often do you allow other people's opinions to dictate your emotional state?

One powerful tool to help you reclaim your energy is **mindfulness**—the practice of staying present in the moment without judgment. When you are mindful, you become aware of where your focus is going and can intentionally bring it back to what truly matters.

I began practicing mindfulness when I realized how often I was letting my mind wander to things I couldn't control. I started small—focusing on my breath for just five minutes a day. Over time, this practice helped me regain control over my thoughts and energy. Instead of being carried away by anxiety or worry, I learned to return to the present moment and focus on what I could actually change.

As **Jon Kabat-Zinn**, the founder of the Mindfulness-Based Stress Reduction program, says:

"You can't stop the waves, but you can learn to surf."

This is the essence of reclaiming your personal power—recognizing that while you can't control every wave in life, you can learn to surf the waves with grace and focus.

Embracing Your Own Authority Over Your Life

Reclaiming your personal power is about stepping into your own **authority**—the realization that you are the one who gets to decide how you show up in the world. No one else has the right to dictate your choices, your path, or your sense of self-worth. When we begin to embrace our own authority, we stop seeking permission from others and take full responsibility for our lives.

I'll never forget the moment when I realized that I had been **waiting for someone else** to tell me I was "good enough" or "worthy." I had spent so many years seeking external validation—waiting for a boss to give me a promotion, waiting for a partner to tell me I was loved, waiting for friends to tell me I was successful. But all of this waiting was keeping me **stuck** in a cycle of insecurity and doubt.

The turning point came when I realized: **I am already enough.** I didn't need anyone else's approval to live a life that felt fulfilling. I was the one who held the authority over my choices and actions. This was a profound realization—it was as though a weight had been lifted from my shoulders.

This concept is perfectly captured in **Audre Lorde's** words:

"I am not free while any woman is unfree, even when her shackles are very different from my own."

This quote speaks to the idea that our freedom comes from within. It's not about the circumstances or the approval of others. It's about reclaiming your own sense of authority and taking responsibility for your life and your decisions.

When we step into our authority, we become **empowered** to create the life we want—whether that's in our relationships, careers, or personal goals. We stop waiting for others to tell us our worth, and we start **defining** our worth for ourselves.

One of the most powerful tools in embracing your own authority is learning to **set boundaries**. Boundaries are the invisible lines that protect your energy and help you prioritize what truly matters. Without boundaries, it's easy to give away your personal power. But when you set clear boundaries, you reclaim the ability to control your time, your energy, and your focus.

For example, I used to say "yes" to every request, even when it didn't align with my values or needs. I was afraid of disappointing people or being seen as "selfish." But over time, I realized that constantly overcommitting was draining my energy and preventing me from focusing on my own goals.

Once I started saying "no" with confidence and setting clear boundaries around my time, I felt a sense of freedom and authority over my life. It was empowering to take control of my schedule and stop giving away my precious energy to things that didn't serve me.

Brené Brown, the research professor and author of *Daring Greatly*, often speaks about the importance of boundaries in living an empowered life:

"Daring to set boundaries is about having the courage to love ourselves, even when we risk disappointing others."

Embracing your authority also involves trusting yourself and your inner wisdom. You don't need to look to others for answers when you begin to trust that you already have the answers within you. This is true **self-leadership**—recognizing that you are the CEO of your own life.

Practical Exercises to Reclaim Your Personal Power

1. **Identify Your Energy Drainers**: Write down a list of activities, people, and situations that drain your energy. Once you have a clear picture, ask yourself: *What can I let go of?* Start by removing or limiting time spent on the things that don't align with your energy and focus.

2. **Practice Mindful Awareness**: Set aside 10 minutes each day to sit quietly and observe your thoughts. Notice when your mind drifts toward worry or stress. Gently bring it back to the present moment. This practice will help you reclaim your focus and energy.

3. **Set Boundaries**: Identify areas in your life where you need to set clearer boundaries. Start small, and practice saying "no" without guilt. Honor your time, your energy, and your needs.

4. **Affirm Your Authority**: Every morning, affirm your power by saying to yourself: *I am in control of my choices and actions. I have the authority to create the life I want.* Repeating this affirmation daily will help you step into your own power.

In the next chapter, we'll dive deeper into how **Letting Them** not only empowers you but also helps you cultivate better relationships, enhance your career, and create a life that aligns with your true values.

This chapter explores how to **reclaim your personal power** by understanding the psychology behind letting go, stopping the giving away of your energy and focus, and embracing your authority over your life. Through personal stories, thought-provoking exercises, and powerful quotes from renowned thinkers, the chapter aims to inspire readers to take responsibility for their happiness and success. The key takeaway is that personal power comes from within and can be cultivated by letting go of control, setting boundaries, and embracing self-trust.

Chapter 4: Letting Go of Other People's Opinions

Why We Care So Much About What Others Think

If you're like most people, you've probably found yourself thinking about what others think of you—whether it's after an interaction with a friend, a colleague, or even a stranger. This tendency to care about others' opinions is deeply ingrained in human nature. From an evolutionary standpoint, our survival once depended on **social acceptance**. The need to belong, to fit in, and to be approved by others was essential for survival in tribal societies. Those who were accepted by the group were more likely to thrive, while those who were ostracized were left vulnerable to the harshness of the environment.

This deep-rooted psychological need for approval from others can be traced back to childhood. Many of us were taught to seek validation from our parents, teachers, or peers. From a young age, we learned that being "liked" and "approved of" was directly linked to our sense of **self-worth**. We internalized the belief that our value as human beings depends on how others perceive us. This is known as **external validation**, and it's one of the most powerful forces that can dictate how we behave, think, and feel.

However, as we grow older, this reliance on others' approval becomes a source of tremendous **stress** and **anxiety**. No matter how much we try to control how others see us, there will always be people who disagree with us, misunderstand us, or even criticize us. And yet, many of us still keep seeking that elusive approval, constantly adjusting our actions and behaviors to win others over.

This was the case for me for many years. I used to be consumed with the idea that I needed to impress people in order to feel good about myself. In social situations, I would find myself scanning the room, gauging others' reactions, wondering if they were judging me, or if I was meeting their expectations. The **constant self-monitoring** was exhausting, and it left me feeling drained, unworthy, and insecure.

One vivid memory that stands out was when I was preparing for a public speaking event. I had a deep fear of how the audience would perceive me, and I spent hours obsessing over every possible detail: my outfit, my tone of voice, the words I used. Even though I had a message I wanted to share, all I could focus on was how people might judge me. I was so fixated on this fear of judgment that I nearly backed out of the event altogether.

When I finally mustered the courage to go on stage, I realized something incredibly liberating: Most people weren't thinking about me at all. They were absorbed in their own thoughts, their own experiences, and their own judgments. The pressure I had placed on myself to be perfect was entirely self-imposed. This experience was a turning point for me. I realized that I had been giving away my power by worrying excessively about what others thought of me. The truth was, **most people aren't paying as much attention to us as we think.**

As **Eleanor Roosevelt** famously said:

"You wouldn't worry so much about what others think of you if you realized how seldom they do."

This quote was a revelation for me. It highlighted the **truth** that people are often far more focused on their own lives than on scrutinizing ours. The mental and emotional energy I had spent worrying about other people's opinions was energy that could have been spent on things that truly mattered to me.

So why do we continue to care about what others think, even when it limits our potential and happiness? The simple answer is that **we're wired** to seek approval. But the more complicated answer lies in our **fear**—fear of rejection, fear of failure, and fear of not being enough. These fears are rooted in our **insecurities**, and when we don't feel secure in ourselves, we look to others for validation.

The Freedom That Comes When You Stop Seeking Approval

Imagine a life where you no longer cared about what others thought of you. A life where you didn't need to impress anyone or gain approval to feel worthy. What would that life look like? **Liberating**, right?

When you let go of the need for external validation, you take back control of your life. You stop being a prisoner of others' opinions, and you start making decisions based on **your own values**, beliefs, and desires. The freedom that comes with this shift is not just emotional—it's transformative.

In my own journey, I began to realize that my **self-worth** couldn't be tied to the approval of others. I started practicing the art of **self-acceptance**, which meant recognizing my worth and value independent of anyone else's opinion. I stopped seeking approval from friends, family, or strangers, and instead, focused on cultivating a relationship of acceptance and love with myself.

One of the ways I did this was by **redefining success**. For so long, I had defined success based on how others saw me. I believed that success meant achieving certain external markers—like getting a promotion, owning a house, or being admired by others. But when I let go of this narrow definition, I found that success could be something much more personal and fulfilling. Success became about living a life true to myself, not one that was built on the expectations of others.

There's a profound sense of **peace** that comes when you stop seeking external approval. No longer do you have to worry about whether people like you, admire you, or agree with you. Instead, you focus on whether you like **yourself** and whether you're living in alignment with your own values and goals.

This concept is beautifully captured by **Wayne Dyer**, who said:

"Self-worth comes from one thing – thinking that you are worthy."

When you stop seeking approval from others, you recognize that your worth is intrinsic—it comes from within. You are worthy simply because you exist, not because you've earned anyone else's approval.

One way to cultivate this internal sense of worth is to practice **self-compassion**. Often, the reason we seek approval is because we don't feel **good enough**. Self-compassion allows us to be kind and understanding toward ourselves, to treat ourselves with the same care and empathy that we would offer to a close friend.

How to Build Unshakable Confidence

Building **unshakable confidence** is a process that requires both internal work and external practice. Confidence doesn't come from the validation of others; it comes from developing a deep trust in yourself. When you stop relying on external approval, you begin to build the kind of confidence that isn't dependent on external circumstances.

1. Cultivate Self-Awareness: The first step in building confidence is understanding yourself—your strengths, your weaknesses, and your values. Self-awareness allows you to recognize your worth without needing others to tell you. When you know who you are and what you stand for, you can walk through life with the confidence that comes from being **authentically you.**

I used to struggle with my own self-awareness. I would often define myself by the roles I played in other people's lives—daughter, friend, partner—rather than by my own intrinsic qualities. It was only when I began to reflect on what made me feel truly alive, what made me passionate, and what I wanted to contribute to the world that I started to build unshakable confidence. I stopped defining myself by the approval of others and started embracing my own identity.

2. Embrace Vulnerability: True confidence isn't about perfection—it's about accepting that you are human, and that imperfection is part of the process. When you embrace your **vulnerabilities**, you free yourself from the need to maintain a facade of perfection. Vulnerability is the key to building deeper connections with others and with yourself. It's about showing up authentically, even if it means risking judgment or rejection.

One of the most powerful lessons I learned was from **Brené Brown**, who is an expert in vulnerability and shame. She said:

"Vulnerability is not winning or losing; it's having the courage to show up and be seen when we have no control over the outcome."

When I started embracing vulnerability in my personal and professional life, I found that people appreciated me more for my **authenticity** than for my attempts at perfection. By allowing myself to be real and imperfect, I built more meaningful and fulfilling relationships.

3. Practice Self-Affirmation: Confidence grows when you consistently affirm your worth. Positive affirmations are powerful tools for reshaping your self-perception. Every day, remind yourself that you are capable, worthy, and deserving of love and success. The more you affirm your value, the more confident you become.

An affirmation that worked wonders for me was: **"I am enough, just as I am."** Repeating this simple statement each morning helped me start the day with confidence, knowing that I didn't need anyone else's approval to feel worthy.

4. Take Bold Action: Confidence is built through experience. The more you step out of your comfort zone and take risks, the more you prove to yourself that you are capable. Every small victory—whether it's speaking up in a meeting or trying something new—builds your self-assurance.

I remember my first time speaking at a large event. I was terrified, but I knew that in order to build the confidence I desired, I had to **take action**. I reminded myself that I wasn't speaking for approval—I was speaking to share my message. The experience was both terrifying and empowering, but it helped me build the kind of confidence that doesn't crumble under pressure.

5. Surround Yourself with Supportive People: Building unshakable confidence requires a supportive environment. Seek out people who encourage you, believe in your potential, and accept you for who you are. These people will help you stay grounded in your own worth and remind you of your strengths when self-doubt creeps in.

Conclusion

Letting go of other people's opinions is one of the most liberating things you can do for your own personal growth. When you stop seeking approval, you reclaim your power, your peace, and your sense of self-worth. You begin to live life on your own terms, making decisions based on what is true for you, rather than what others expect from you. As you build unshakable confidence, you learn to trust yourself and embrace your uniqueness, knowing that you are worthy of love and success, no matter what anyone else thinks.

In the next chapter, we'll explore how to **cultivate resilience**—the ability to bounce back from setbacks and stay true to your vision, even when faced with challenges.

Key Takeaways:

- **We care about others' opinions because we've been conditioned to seek approval.**

- **The freedom that comes from letting go of approval-seeking is transformative.**

- **Unshakable confidence is built on self-awareness, vulnerability, self-affirmation, bold action, and supportive relationships.**

Quotes to Remember:

- "You wouldn't worry so much about what others think of you if you realized how seldom they do." **— Eleanor Roosevelt**

- "Self-worth comes from one thing – thinking that you are worthy." **— Wayne Dyer**

- "Vulnerability is not winning or losing; it's having the courage to show up and be seen when we have no control over the outcome." **— Brené Brown**

Chapter 5: Letting Go of the Drama

How to Release the Emotional Weight of Other People's Drama

Drama is something that many people are intimately familiar with—it can feel as if you're constantly caught in a whirlwind of emotions, conflicts, and situations that are completely out of your control. But if we're being honest, much of the drama that weighs us down is **not our own**. It's often the emotional baggage of those around us. Family members, friends, coworkers, and even strangers can bring drama into our lives, and it's easy to get entangled in their stories.

I learned this lesson in my own life, the hard way. For a long time, I thought that being a **supportive friend** or a **good partner** meant taking on other people's emotional burdens. I'd listen to a friend vent about her stressful day at work, and I would feel obligated to take on her frustrations. A colleague would unload about office politics, and I'd give advice and try to solve problems. A family member would share a long list of grievances about their relationship, and I'd feel as though it was my responsibility to help them fix it. The problem? I ended up absorbing all of these emotions, wearing them like a cloak over my own well-being.

One of the most **defining moments** of this realization came after a long conversation with a friend who was going through a difficult breakup. She'd been struggling with her feelings of rejection and anger, and every time we spoke, it felt like I was diving into the emotional deep end with her. I empathized with her deeply, but at some point, it became clear that I wasn't just **feeling for her**; I was feeling **with her**—her pain became my pain. After the conversation ended, I found myself physically drained, anxious, and agitated. I wasn't able to process my own feelings because I was too caught up in hers.

At that point, I realized that **empathy is a gift**, but there's a fine line between **empathizing** and becoming emotionally entangled in someone else's drama. It's one thing to lend an ear and offer support; it's another to let their problems consume you. When you start carrying the emotional weight of someone else's situation, it's no longer **support**—it's codependence.

The first step in releasing this emotional weight is **acknowledging** that their drama doesn't belong to you. This recognition is incredibly freeing because it gives you permission to separate your emotions from theirs.

Here are a few ways to begin releasing that emotional weight:

1. **Recognize the difference between empathy and enmeshment**: Empathy is the ability to understand and share someone else's feelings, but **enmeshment** occurs when you start losing yourself in their emotions. It's important to recognize when you are no longer just a

supportive friend but are actively absorbing someone else's stress, pain, or anxiety.

2. **Develop emotional detachment**: Emotional detachment doesn't mean you stop caring—it means you no longer let other people's emotional chaos dictate your emotional state. When someone brings drama into your life, practice **observing it** instead of emotionally reacting to it. It's like watching a storm roll in from a distance—you can see it, acknowledge it, but you don't have to stand in the rain.

3. **Recognize your emotional triggers**: Notice when someone's story or situation starts triggering your emotions. For example, if you're talking to someone who's constantly upset about work, and you start feeling **anxious** or **angry**, pause for a moment. Ask yourself, *Is this my feeling? Or is this someone else's drama seeping into my emotions?*

4. **Practice emotional self-care**: After you engage in a conversation that involves a lot of emotional drama, take time to **clear your own emotional space**. You might need to meditate, journal, or even take a walk to decompress. Practice grounding techniques to reconnect with your own energy and shed the emotional weight.

5. **Acknowledge your limits**: Understand that you can't fix everything. If you find yourself trying to "solve" the problem for someone, take a step back and ask yourself, *Am I offering helpful*

advice, or am I trying to take responsibility for their emotions?

Eckhart Tolle wisely says:

"Whatever you think the world is withholding from you, you are withholding from the world."

When we hold onto the drama of others, we are withholding our own peace, energy, and inner joy. We cannot be of true help to others if we are depleted by their emotional weight. Releasing the emotional weight allows us to be fully present for others without losing ourselves.

Building Healthy Boundaries That Protect Your Peace

Building boundaries is not about being cold or distant—it's about being **clear** about where your responsibility ends and where someone else's begins. Boundaries are essential to creating space for your own well-being while maintaining healthy, loving relationships with others. When we fail to set boundaries, we often end up **people-pleasing**, saying yes when we should say no, and ultimately allowing others to dictate how we feel and what we do.

A good example from my own life: I once had a close friend who was going through a tumultuous period in her life. She was in an unhealthy relationship, and it seemed like she constantly needed emotional support. I found myself taking phone calls late into the night, trying to give advice, and often feeling emotionally drained afterward. In my mind, I was being **supportive**, but over time, it became clear that my friend's problems were consuming more of my emotional bandwidth than they should have been. The more I tried to "help," the more she seemed to need me, and the more exhausted I felt.

Eventually, I had to take a hard look at the situation and ask myself: *Am I truly helping her, or am I enabling her to remain stuck in her pain?* I realized that **by not setting boundaries**, I was allowing her to monopolize my time and energy. I had to learn how to gently but firmly set limits.

Here's how you can begin to set healthy boundaries that protect your peace:

1. **Know your limits**: You cannot give what you don't have. If you are emotionally exhausted or overwhelmed, it's okay to step back. Set limits on how much time and energy you can invest in other people's problems.

2. **Communicate clearly**: Boundaries require clear communication. You can say things like, *"I'm happy to listen, but I need to keep this conversation to 30 minutes so I can stay focused on my own priorities,"* or *"I'm sorry, but I can't offer you any more advice on this situation right now. I need to focus on other things."*

3. **Don't feel guilty**: Guilt often accompanies boundary-setting, especially if you're someone

who is naturally empathetic or people-pleasing. However, setting boundaries isn't selfish—it's necessary for your mental and emotional well-being. Remember: **You can't pour from an empty cup.**

4. **Be firm but kind**: It's important to set boundaries in a way that is respectful, but also firm. If someone continues to overstep your boundaries, you may need to reaffirm them by saying something like, *"I know this is difficult for you, but I need to take a break from this conversation."*

5. **Learn to say no**: Saying no is a vital part of boundary-setting. You don't have to justify your decision. Simply saying, *"I'm not able to do that,"* or *"That doesn't work for me right now,"* is enough. It's not about being dismissive; it's about respecting your own time and energy.

As **Brené Brown** reminds us:

"Daring to set boundaries is about having the courage to love ourselves, even when we risk disappointing others."

Setting boundaries doesn't just protect you—it also creates healthier relationships, where both parties can respect each other's space and needs.

Understanding What You Can—and Can't—Control in Relationships

One of the greatest sources of emotional stress is our desire to control the behavior or emotions of others. The truth is, you can **only control yourself**—not your partner, your friends, your colleagues, or anyone else. Understanding what is within your control and what is not is crucial in releasing the weight of other people's drama.

Take, for example, a relationship I had where I was constantly trying to change my partner's behavior. He had certain habits and tendencies that drove me crazy, and I thought if I just explained things enough, he would "see the light" and change. I would spend countless hours trying to make him see things my way, but all I was doing was creating tension and frustration. The truth was, I could not control his actions or decisions— only my own reactions.

In order to find peace, I had to learn that **control is an illusion**. The only person you can control in any relationship is yourself. When you let go of the need to control others, you can focus on what truly matters: your own growth, your own happiness, and your own well-being.

To start letting go of the need to control:

1. **Accept that people will act according to their own beliefs and patterns**: You cannot change someone's behavior unless they choose to. The

best thing you can do is to focus on how you respond, not on trying to change others.

2. **Focus on your own growth**: Rather than trying to fix someone else, focus on developing yourself. How can you show up as the best version of yourself in the relationship?

3. **Let go of expectations**: When you release the expectation that people will behave in a certain way, you stop setting yourself up for disappointment.

Conclusion: The Freedom of Letting Go of Drama

Letting go of the emotional weight of other people's drama is a powerful way to reclaim your peace and protect your energy. It's not about abandoning others— it's about recognizing your own limits and setting boundaries that allow you to engage with others without losing yourself. By understanding what you can and can't control, practicing emotional detachment, and learning to set healthy boundaries, you can free yourself from the chaos of other people's emotions and create a more peaceful, fulfilling life.

As **Wayne Dyer** so eloquently put it:

"You cannot always control what goes on outside, but you can always control what goes on inside."

By letting go of the drama, you create the space to focus on what truly matters: your own happiness, your growth, and your peace.

Key Takeaways:

- **Drama is not yours to carry**—release the emotional weight of other people's problems.

- **Healthy boundaries** are essential for preserving your peace and emotional well-being.

- **You cannot control others**—but you can control your reactions and set boundaries that protect your energy.

Quotes to Remember:

- "Whatever you think the world is withholding from you, you are withholding from the world." **— Eckhart Tolle**

- "Daring to set boundaries is about having the courage to love ourselves, even when we risk disappointing others." **— Brené Brown**

- "You cannot always control what goes on outside, but you can always control what goes on inside." **— Wayne Dyer**

Chapter 6: Letting Go of Fear and Self-Doubt

Why Fear Keeps You Stuck in the Cycle of Trying to Control Everything

Fear is often the root cause of our inability to let go of control. It is the invisible force that keeps us tethered to the idea that we must manage every aspect of our lives—whether it's our career, our relationships, or our personal growth. At its core, fear is the belief that something bad might happen if we stop controlling things. But when we live in constant fear, we create a cycle that only amplifies our anxiety and stress. We overextend ourselves, trying to manage things we cannot control, and the result is exhaustion, burnout, and a lack of fulfillment.

I remember a time when I was starting my first business. The fear of failure was overwhelming, and I believed that if I didn't keep a firm grip on every single detail, everything would collapse. I was micromanaging every task, checking up on employees constantly, and trying to forecast every possible outcome of a project. I couldn't delegate; I couldn't trust others to do things to my level of perfection. It was paralyzing.

One night, after a particularly stressful day of trying to control every element of a new launch, I found myself sitting at my desk at 2 a.m., utterly spent. I had made little progress on my actual goals, and all my energy had been wasted managing things that I simply couldn't control. That night, I realized that my fear of failure was keeping me trapped in a cycle of over-control. I was so afraid of making mistakes that I couldn't allow myself to move forward.

This experience was the catalyst for my understanding that **fear of failure is often a mask for the fear of not being enough**. We try to control everything because, on some deep level, we believe that if we don't, we'll be judged, criticized, or rejected. This fear of judgment makes us doubt ourselves and our abilities.

But the reality is that **perfectionism and over-control are not the solution to fear**; they only perpetuate the cycle of self-doubt and anxiety.

As **Brené Brown** puts it:

"Perfectionism is not the key to success. It's the avoidance of failure. But it's also the biggest trap, because in trying to avoid failure, we miss the opportunity for growth and authenticity."

Fear and self-doubt keep us stuck because they don't allow us to fully embrace our vulnerabilities, which are actually the places where growth and strength lie. The key to breaking the cycle of fear and control is to **accept that we cannot control everything**, and that is perfectly okay. The moment we stop trying to control outcomes, we free ourselves to engage more fully in the process of living.

How to Stop Second-Guessing Yourself and Trust Your Inner Voice

Second-guessing yourself is one of the most common manifestations of self-doubt. When you are constantly doubting your decisions, you undermine your own confidence and your ability to trust your instincts. Self-doubt robs you of your **inner authority** and forces you to seek external validation, often from people who may not understand your journey or your desires.

I have struggled with second-guessing myself more times than I can count. In the early days of my career, I would find myself ruminating on decisions I had made, wondering if I was doing the right thing, and seeking reassurance from others. Should I take that new job? Should I launch that new project? Is this the right path for me? The constant **back-and-forth** left me exhausted, and I would often feel like I was in limbo, unable to make progress because I was too afraid of making a mistake.

I remember once, I was offered a big opportunity to collaborate on a project that seemed like a perfect fit for me. I was excited about the possibilities, but the more I thought about it, the more I doubted myself. *Would I be able to deliver? What if I wasn't good enough? What if people didn't like my ideas?* These thoughts paralyzed me. I realized that the more I second-guessed myself, the less action I took, and the further away I got from my goals.

That was when I began to practice **tuning into my inner voice**—the part of me that knew the answer long before my head started to overthink it. Instead of obsessing over the "what-ifs," I started to trust my intuition and make decisions from a place of alignment rather than fear. This shift didn't happen overnight, but every time I acted on my inner knowing, the doubts began to dissipate.

How can you stop second-guessing yourself and start trusting your inner voice?

1. **Practice self-awareness**: The first step is to tune into your internal dialogue. Notice when you begin to question your decisions or when you feel overwhelmed by doubt. The more you become aware of these patterns, the easier it will be to interrupt them.

2. **Cultivate self-compassion**: Instead of berating yourself for not knowing the "perfect" answer right away, practice self-compassion. It's okay to not have everything figured out. Trust that you are doing the best you can with the information you have.

3. **Start small**: If you're overwhelmed by big decisions, start by making smaller ones and practice trusting yourself. Each time you make a decision and act on it, your self-trust will grow.

4. **Lean into discomfort**: Trusting your inner voice can feel uncomfortable at first, especially if you're used to relying on external validation. But

discomfort is often a sign that you're growing. Don't shy away from it.

5. **Let go of the need for external validation**: When you stop seeking approval from others, you free yourself from the cycle of second-guessing. Trust that your own opinion is the only one that matters when it comes to your decisions.

Oprah Winfrey offers a powerful perspective on this:

"The biggest adventure you can take is to live the life of your dreams."

To live that adventure, you have to trust yourself and your own instincts. Your inner voice is a guide—listen to it, and the path will reveal itself.

Overcoming Imposter Syndrome with the Let Them Mindset

Imposter syndrome is the pervasive feeling that you are a fraud, that you don't deserve your success, or that you're not "good enough" despite evidence to the contrary. It can show up in subtle ways, like feeling like you're just lucky or that you've somehow "fooled" people into thinking you're competent. **Imposter syndrome often keeps us trapped in a cycle of self-doubt, preventing us from fully embracing our accomplishments and abilities.**

I struggled with imposter syndrome early in my career. Every time I received praise for a project or a job well done, a little voice in my head would whisper, *You don't deserve this. You're not qualified. You're just faking it.* I would look at people who I admired and thought, *They are so much more experienced and knowledgeable than I am. How can I possibly compare?*

This feeling of being "less-than" kept me in a cycle of **overcompensating**—working longer hours, going above and beyond, but never feeling truly satisfied with my efforts. I had convinced myself that I needed to "prove" my worth at every turn, constantly worried that someone would discover I wasn't as capable as they thought.

The **Let Them mindset** played a pivotal role in overcoming my imposter syndrome. By letting go of the need to control other people's perceptions of me, I realized that my worth was not determined by their judgments. The truth is, **other people's opinions are none of your business**. The Let Them mindset is about freeing yourself from the suffocating belief that you need to "prove" your value and instead trusting in your own path and process.

How can the Let Them mindset help you overcome imposter syndrome?

1. **Let go of the need for external validation**: If you're waiting for someone else to tell you that you're good enough, you're giving away your

power. The more you let go of seeking approval, the more you can step into your own confidence.

2. **Recognize that everyone starts somewhere**: Nobody, not even the most successful person you admire, started as an expert. We all start as beginners, and learning is part of the journey. Allow yourself to be a work in progress.

3. **Celebrate your successes**: Acknowledge your achievements, no matter how small. Each success, whether it's finishing a project or receiving positive feedback, is evidence of your ability and growth. You are not a fraud—you are an active participant in your own success.

4. **Embrace mistakes as learning opportunities**: Rather than seeing mistakes as evidence of inadequacy, view them as opportunities for growth. Imposter syndrome thrives on perfectionism, but the Let Them mindset invites you to embrace imperfection and see it as part of the process.

Sheryl Sandberg writes in her book *Lean In*:

"What would you do if you weren't afraid?"

When you stop being afraid of judgment, failure, and mistakes, you create the freedom to step into your full potential. The Let Them mindset helps you overcome imposter syndrome by letting go of the idea that you need to "prove" yourself to others. You are worthy, capable, and deserving of all your success—and you don't need anyone else's approval to validate that.

Conclusion: The Power of Letting Go of Fear and Self-Doubt

Fear and self-doubt are powerful forces, but they don't have to control your life. When you let go of the need to control everything, you create space for trust—trust in yourself, trust in your process, and trust in your ability to navigate uncertainty. The Let Them mindset is about releasing fear and embracing the unknown, knowing that you are capable of handling whatever comes your way.

By learning to stop second-guessing yourself and trusting your inner voice, you open up new possibilities for growth and success. And by overcoming imposter syndrome, you can step into your true potential without the weight of self-doubt holding you back.

Remember: **You are not a fraud. You are not a mistake. You are enough**. Trust in yourself, let go of the fear, and move forward with confidence.

Key Takeaways:

- **Fear keeps you stuck in the cycle of control.** Letting go of fear is essential for breaking free from the need to manage everything.

- **Second-guessing yourself drains your energy**. Practice trusting your inner voice and making decisions from a place of alignment.

- **Imposter syndrome is an illusion**. You are worthy and capable, and you don't need to prove yourself to anyone.

Quotes to Remember:

- "Perfectionism is not the key to success. It's the avoidance of failure. But it's also the biggest trap." — **Brené Brown**

- "The biggest adventure you can take is to live the life of your dreams." — **Oprah Winfrey**

- "What would you do if you weren't afraid?" — **Sheryl Sandberg**

Chapter 7: Letting Go of Perfectionism

The Paradox of Perfection: Why It's Holding You Back

Perfectionism can be a double-edged sword. At first glance, it seems like a noble pursuit. We often equate perfectionism with high standards, diligence, and an unyielding commitment to excellence. In a world that prizes achievement, perfectionism appears to be a mark of success. However, when we peel back the layers, we find that perfectionism is not only a barrier to progress but also a silent saboteur of our personal happiness and growth.

Perfectionism is insidious. It creeps into our lives under the guise of ambition and desire for excellence, yet it prevents us from ever feeling "good enough." It often arises from deep-rooted fears: the fear of judgment, the fear of failure, and the fear of being vulnerable. For many of us, **perfectionism is an attempt to gain control over our uncertain world**, to ensure that nothing we do can be criticized, rejected, or devalued. Yet, ironically, the pursuit of perfection leaves us feeling anxious, exhausted, and disillusioned.

I know this from firsthand experience. For years, I lived in the grip of perfectionism. As a child, I was praised for being meticulous, for getting straight A's, and for achieving high standards. But as I entered adulthood, I realized that my relentless drive for perfection had become a hindrance, not a help. Whether I was working on a presentation, launching a project, or even planning a personal event, I couldn't shake the belief that **every detail had to be flawless**. I would obsess over every decision, constantly tweaking, revising, and second-guessing myself. Even when a project was "finished," I would look for ways to improve it or wonder if I could have done something differently.

One of the most vivid moments where perfectionism held me back was during the early days of my business. I was preparing to launch a new product line, and instead of trusting my team and moving forward, I got bogged down in **minor details**—the packaging, the marketing copy, the social media images. I thought I had to get every aspect of the launch "perfect" before releasing it to the public. This paralysis by analysis delayed the project for weeks, and the opportunity was lost.

It wasn't until I realized that my perfectionism was the true obstacle that I began to change my mindset. The paradox of perfectionism is that while you think it will make you better, it actually **keeps you stuck in a cycle of inaction**. You're afraid to fail, and as a result, you fail to act at all.

The truth is, perfectionism is rooted in fear. Fear of not being enough. Fear of judgment. Fear of being vulnerable. But **perfectionism is the enemy of progress**, and the longer we remain trapped in its grip, the more we hold ourselves back from achieving our potential.

In the words of **Brené Brown**:

"Perfectionism is not the path to success; it's the path to fear, shame, and anxiety. The only way to deal with perfectionism is to confront it head-on and embrace imperfection."

Understanding that perfectionism isn't a mark of success but a form of self-sabotage is the first step toward reclaiming your power and moving toward the life you truly want.

How to Embrace Imperfection and Move Forward with Confidence

Letting go of perfectionism is not about lowering your standards or abandoning your desire for excellence. It's about recognizing that **perfection is an illusion**, and that striving for it often causes more harm than good. Embracing imperfection doesn't mean you stop caring about the quality of your work; it means you release the need for everything to be flawless in order to feel worthy, valuable, or successful.

The process of embracing imperfection is a journey—one that requires **self-compassion, mindfulness, and courage**. Here's how you can start:

1. **Recognize Perfectionism for What It Is**: The first step is becoming aware of the ways perfectionism shows up in your life. Do you avoid starting a project because you fear you won't do it perfectly? Do you obsess over small details that don't ultimately matter? Do you procrastinate because you're waiting for the "right" time or the perfect conditions? Recognizing these patterns is the first step toward breaking free.

2. **Challenge the Fear of Imperfection**: Ask yourself: What's the worst thing that can happen if something isn't perfect? Often, our fear of imperfection is more about how we perceive others' reactions than the actual consequences. Will people really judge you harshly if your work isn't flawless? Or will they appreciate the effort, creativity, and authenticity behind it? The truth is, most people are too busy with their own lives to scrutinize your every move. In fact, vulnerability and imperfection are often the very things that create authentic connection.

3. **Shift Your Focus from Perfection to Progress**: Perfectionism often stems from the desire to control the outcome, but true success comes from **progress, not perfection**. Instead of focusing on getting everything perfect from the start, shift your attention to the process of learning and growing. Celebrate every small step forward, no matter how imperfect. Progress, however messy, is the key to moving forward and achieving your goals.

4. **Be Kind to Yourself**: Letting go of perfectionism requires **self-compassion**. When you make a mistake or fall short of your expectations, don't beat yourself up. Instead, practice kindness. Remind yourself that you are human, and it's okay to make mistakes. In fact, mistakes are opportunities to learn and improve. You wouldn't expect a child learning to walk to do so perfectly, so why hold yourself to a higher standard?

5. **Give Yourself Permission to Fail**: Failure isn't the enemy—**it's part of the journey**. When we allow ourselves the freedom to fail, we give ourselves permission to experiment, take risks, and try new things. Failure doesn't define you; your ability to rise from it does. Embrace failure as a stepping stone on the path to growth and success.

I learned this lesson the hard way in my own life. I used to fear failure so much that I avoided taking risks altogether. But once I realized that the fear of failure was keeping me stuck, I started taking small steps to embrace imperfection. I allowed myself to release work that wasn't "perfect" and to move forward even when I wasn't sure I had everything figured out. And with each imperfect step, I grew stronger and more confident.

Steve Jobs once said:

"Your work is going to fill a large part of your life, and the only way to be truly satisfied is to do what you believe is great work. And the only way to do great work is to love what you do."

Loving what you do means giving yourself permission to be imperfect, to make mistakes, and to continue learning. It means valuing the journey of progress over the pursuit of perfection.

The Power of Progress Over Perfection

The notion that **progress is more important than perfection** is liberating. It shifts the focus from an unattainable standard to the attainable goal of continuous improvement. When you make progress your measure of success, you stop holding yourself back with fear and self-doubt. You begin to take action, even if that action isn't perfect.

One of the most powerful examples of this principle in action comes from the world of **creativity**. Artists, writers, and entrepreneurs all face the tension between wanting their work to be perfect and knowing that they need to make progress in order to succeed. Some of the most successful people in history have embraced the idea that **imperfection is the gateway to growth**.

Take **J.K. Rowling**, for example. When she wrote *Harry Potter and the Sorcerer's Stone*, she had no idea it would become a global phenomenon. She had no guarantees, no blueprint for success. In fact, her manuscript was rejected by multiple publishers before it finally found a home. If Rowling had allowed perfectionism to dictate her progress, she might never have written the book at all. Instead, she focused on creating the best version of the story she could, knowing that her work would evolve over time.

Similarly, **Thomas Edison** is famously quoted as saying:

"I have not failed. I've just found 10,000 ways that won't work."

Edison's journey was not about perfection—it was about trial, error, and learning through doing. The idea that progress is more important than perfection was essential to his success. If Edison had waited for the "perfect" lightbulb design before launching, we might still be in the dark.

Conclusion: Embracing Imperfection for a Fuller Life

Letting go of perfectionism is not about lowering your standards or abandoning your goals. It's about embracing the journey of progress—**moving forward with confidence, knowing that imperfections are part of the process**. By focusing on progress, not perfection, you free yourself from the burden of constant self-criticism and open up new possibilities for growth and creativity.

Progress, not perfection, is the key to living a fulfilling and successful life. It's about making steady steps forward, learning from mistakes, and valuing the process over the outcome.

As **Albert Einstein** once said:

"Strive not to be a success, but rather to be of value."

When you focus on progress rather than perfection, you start to create value in everything you do. You let go of the pressure to be flawless and instead allow yourself to evolve, to grow, and to create with confidence.

Key Takeaways:

- **Perfectionism is a barrier to progress.** It creates fear, self-doubt, and procrastination, holding you back from taking action.

- **Embrace imperfection.** Allow yourself to fail, learn, and grow. Perfection is an illusion; progress is the key to success.

- **Shift your focus from perfection to progress.** Celebrate the journey and take pride in the steps you take toward your goals, even if they're imperfect.

- **Be kind to yourself.** Practice self-compassion, and remind yourself that mistakes are opportunities for growth.

Quotes to Remember:

- **"Perfectionism is not the path to success; it's the path to fear, shame, and anxiety."** — Brené Brown

- "Your work is going to fill a large part of your life, and the only way to be truly satisfied is to do what you believe is great work." — Steve Jobs

- "I have not failed. I've just found 10,000 ways that won't work." — Thomas Edison

- "Strive not to be a success, but rather to be of value." — Albert Einstein

Chapter 8: Letting Go of Comparison

How Constantly Comparing Yourself to Others Sabotages Your Success

Comparison is a silent thief of joy. It's a subtle force that creeps into our thoughts, often without us even realizing it. In today's hyper-connected world, where social media constantly bombards us with curated glimpses of other people's lives, it's easy to fall into the trap of comparing ourselves to others. We look at someone else's achievements, appearance, or lifestyle and start to feel as though we're falling short.

But here's the hard truth: **Constantly comparing yourself to others is one of the most destructive things you can do for your success and happiness**. It not only distracts you from your own goals, but it also undermines your self-worth and confidence.

I've experienced this firsthand. For years, I measured my success by comparing myself to others. Whether it was looking at the success of my peers in the industry, comparing my body to the images I saw on social media, or even comparing my life to what I thought it "should" look like, I was constantly making myself feel inadequate.

One of the most memorable instances came when I first started my own business. I had recently left a stable job and was launching a new product. Initially, I felt so excited and proud of my decision. But as the days passed, I began to scroll through social media, seeing my peers' posts about their own businesses, their lavish vacations, their partnerships with influencers. I couldn't help but think: *"Why is their business thriving while mine seems to be moving at a snail's pace?"* I'd start comparing my "behind-the-scenes" to their "highlight reels," and before I knew it, I was questioning my worth, my ability, and my decision to even start this journey.

The problem with comparison is that it's never based on the full picture. When we compare ourselves to others, we often compare our worst day to someone else's best. We're looking at a snapshot of someone else's life—whether it's their success, their happiness, or their achievements—and forgetting that we have no idea what's going on behind the scenes.

As **Theodore Roosevelt** famously said, **"Comparison is the thief of joy."** This quote hit me like a ton of bricks when I first heard it. It perfectly summed up the feeling I had whenever I compared myself to others—my joy was stolen, and in its place, I was left with frustration, self-doubt, and resentment.

What I realized over time is that comparison does nothing but erode our self-esteem. Instead of motivating us to improve, it leads to a cycle of **self-criticism and unproductive envy**. The constant need to measure up to others prevents us from staying focused on our own journey, and it makes it harder to celebrate our own wins, no matter how small.

The act of comparison also sends a message that we don't trust our own abilities, that we need to be like someone else to be good enough. But we are not meant to replicate someone else's success. We are meant to chart our own path, and that requires a deep level of self-awareness and confidence—something comparison only steals away.

The Danger of Measuring Your Worth by Other People's Standards

When we compare ourselves to others, we are, in essence, measuring our worth by someone else's standards. This creates a dangerous cycle of external validation, where our sense of self is entirely dependent on how we stack up against others. We start to believe that our value is determined by external achievements, societal expectations, or the validation we receive from others.

For much of my early career, I lived by the standards of others. I would look at my colleagues and peers—people whose careers seemed to be progressing faster or who had more recognition—and ask myself, *"Why am I not there yet?"* The problem was, I was measuring my progress by someone else's yardstick.

There's a powerful story about **Jim Carrey** that illustrates this point beautifully. Carrey is known for his success in Hollywood, but his early career was fraught with doubt. At one point, he wrote himself a check for **$10 million** and dated it for Thanksgiving 1995. He kept that check in his wallet, visualizing his success. When he was finally paid **$10 million** for his role in *Dumb and Dumber*, it wasn't because he had focused on competing with others. It was because he believed in his own unique journey and stayed true to his path.

Had Carrey spent his time comparing himself to other actors or measuring his success against theirs, he might have given up before he even reached his big break. Instead, he focused on his own growth and stayed true to his vision. **He created success on his own terms**, rather than trying to meet someone else's standard of success.

When we measure our worth by someone else's standards, we are outsourcing our sense of value. We make our happiness conditional on external factors—whether it's the approval of others, the number of followers we have, or how well we are doing in comparison to our peers. The problem is that **external standards are fleeting**. As soon as we achieve one milestone, we move the goalposts further away in order to match someone else's success. And the cycle continues.

The real danger of comparison is that it shifts our focus from what truly matters—our own goals, our own values, and our own unique journey—to something external that is often out of our control.

Shifting Your Focus from Competition to Cooperation

Rather than competing with others, we need to shift our mindset from **competition to cooperation**. Instead of seeing others as threats to our success, we can choose to see them as allies, mentors, or sources of inspiration.

This shift is powerful. It transforms the feeling of scarcity—where we think there is only so much success to go around—into an abundance mindset, where we realize that success isn't a limited resource. There's enough for everyone, and we all have the potential to achieve our goals in our own time, in our own way.

Cooperation encourages collaboration over competition. It allows us to acknowledge and celebrate the achievements of others without feeling threatened by them. Rather than comparing ourselves to others, we can learn from them, be inspired by their journey, and use their success as fuel to keep moving forward on our own path.

I saw this principle in action when I connected with a mentor during a particularly challenging time in my career. I was feeling stuck and disillusioned, overwhelmed by the success of others in my field. But my mentor reminded me that success is not a zero-sum game. Instead of focusing on what others had that I didn't, she encouraged me to **collaborate** with those I admired. She suggested I reach out to people in my industry, not as competitors, but as peers to learn from and work with.

One of the most rewarding collaborations I had was with a fellow entrepreneur who had an entirely different approach to business. Instead of viewing him as someone to compete with, I asked for his advice and we worked together on a joint project. The results were far greater than what I could have achieved alone. **By focusing on cooperation instead of comparison, we both grew and succeeded in ways that we couldn't have done by working alone.**

Shifting from competition to cooperation can be the key to unlocking more success in your own life. You don't need to beat others to win. In fact, cooperation fosters innovation, creativity, and growth, which ultimately leads to greater success for everyone involved.

As **Oprah Winfrey** famously said:

"I don't believe in competition. I believe in collaboration."

How to Stop Comparing Yourself to Others: Practical Tips for a Fulfilling Life

1. **Recognize the Comparison Trap**: The first step is simply becoming aware of when you're

comparing yourself to others. When you catch yourself scrolling through social media and feeling inadequate, take a moment to pause. Recognize that what you're seeing isn't the full picture, and remind yourself that your journey is yours alone.

2. **Practice Gratitude**: One of the best ways to combat comparison is by practicing gratitude. Shift your focus from what you lack to what you have. Focus on your own accomplishments, no matter how small, and recognize the progress you've made. Keep a gratitude journal, and every day, write down three things you're thankful for. This simple practice helps you build a positive mindset that sees your life as abundant, rather than lacking.

3. **Unfollow Social Media Accounts That Trigger Comparison**: If you find yourself feeling inadequate after looking at someone else's posts on social media, consider unfollowing or muting those accounts. Your mental health is more important than keeping up with someone else's life. Create a social media environment that supports your well-being and focuses on positivity, inspiration, and growth.

4. **Celebrate Other People's Success**: Instead of feeling jealous or resentful when someone else achieves something you want, choose to celebrate their success. See it as proof that it's possible and use it as motivation. **When we celebrate others, we break free from the trap**

of comparison and replace it with a mindset of abundance and possibility.

5. **Focus on Your Own Goals**: Define what success means to you—not what it means to someone else. Create a vision for your life based on your values, your passions, and your goals. Spend your energy working toward those goals, and trust that success will come at the right time.

Conclusion: Your Journey is Unique

Letting go of comparison is one of the most empowering things you can do for your mental health and your personal success. It frees you from the prison of external validation and allows you to focus on what truly matters—your own growth, your own achievements, and your own journey.

Comparison is a thief of joy, but it's also a thief of success. It keeps you stuck in a cycle of self-doubt and frustration, preventing you from moving forward with confidence. The real key to success is **cooperation, not competition**, and understanding that there is no one path to greatness—there are many. The only measure of success that truly matters is **your own progress**, and by shifting your focus away from comparing yourself to others, you free yourself to create the life you've always wanted.

Key Takeaways:

- **Comparison is the thief of joy.** It robs you of the ability to appreciate your own progress and unique journey.

- **Measuring your worth by other people's standards** is a dangerous cycle that keeps you from realizing your full potential.

- **Shift from competition to cooperation.** Celebrate others' successes as inspiration rather than threats, and collaborate to reach new heights.

- **Focus on your own path and goals.** Define success on your own terms and trust that your journey is uniquely yours.

Quotes to Remember:

- **"Comparison is the thief of joy." — Theodore Roosevelt**

- **"I don't believe in competition. I believe in collaboration." — Oprah Winfrey**

- **"You are your only competition." — Anonymous**

Chapter 9: Letting Go in Your Career

1. Introduction: The Struggle of Control in the Workplace

One of the hardest lessons I had to learn in my career was that the more I tried to control, the more I lost control. The more I clung to my need for perfection, the further away I got from achieving real success. Like many driven individuals, I thought that success meant managing every detail and having my hands on everything—after all, no one cares about your career as much as you do, right?

But over time, the stress became unbearable. I found myself working 12-hour days, sending emails at midnight, staying late at the office, and constantly feeling overwhelmed. The very act of trying to control every aspect of my work was eroding my happiness, creativity, and most importantly—my health.

It was during a pivotal project early in my career that I first saw the cost of this mindset. The project was high-profile, and I took it upon myself to micromanage every step. From reviewing every email before it was sent to making sure every person followed my exact instructions, I was deeply entrenched in the belief that if I didn't oversee everything, things would fall apart.

In the end, not only did the project suffer (because of my inability to delegate), but my team was frustrated, my creativity was stifled, and my own well-being deteriorated. I realized that the very traits that I thought would guarantee success—control and perfectionism—were in fact hindering my growth.

That experience changed me. I had to confront the truth: **letting go of control was the only way forward**. Paradoxically, it was in releasing control that I began to gain it—not only over my career but also over my own happiness and success.

2. The Myth of Micromanagement

Micromanagement is often seen as a badge of perfectionism. It's the belief that no one can do the work as well as you can, so you must oversee every detail. Many people, especially those in leadership positions, feel the overwhelming need to control every facet of their team's work. But the reality is, **micromanagement isn't leadership—it's insecurity**.

At its core, micromanagement stems from fear—the fear that if you let go, the work will fall short of your standards or the outcome will be less than perfect. In my early career, I was caught in this cycle, believing that the only way to ensure the success of my work and my projects was to **control every variable**.

But in trying to control everything, I was actually stifling growth. I wasn't giving others the chance to showcase their talents, and I wasn't fostering an environment where innovation and creativity could thrive.

Steve Jobs, who was known for his intense drive and perfectionism, once said:

"It doesn't make sense to hire smart people and then tell them what to do. We hire smart people so they can tell us what to do."

This quote stuck with me, and it became clear: **Micromanaging others doesn't just waste your time—it wastes their potential**. I was trying to be the gatekeeper to perfection, but in doing so, I was limiting the possibilities that could emerge when I trusted others.

Micromanagement doesn't just harm the team—it harms the person doing the managing as well. The more you try to control, the more stressed and exhausted you become, and the more you sabotage the very success you're working so hard to achieve.

3. Letting Go of Perfectionism in Your Career

Perfectionism is a silent killer of creativity. For years, I believed that perfection was the gold standard, the ultimate goal. If a project wasn't perfect, then I hadn't done my best. I would pour over every detail, double-check every report, rewrite every email.

But perfectionism isn't just about high standards; it's about fear. Fear of failure. Fear of being judged. The more I tried to perfect every single detail, the more I ended up procrastinating or, worse, never finishing anything at all.

Here's the thing: **perfection doesn't exist**, and the constant pursuit of it robs you of your potential. Instead of obsessing over flaws, I realized that progress—not perfection—is what drives success. It was through letting go of perfectionism that I began to see growth in my career and, more importantly, in my own personal development.

I once worked with a team on a new marketing campaign for a major product launch. I had a very clear vision of what it should look like, and I found myself tweaking the smallest details over and over again. It was a beautiful campaign, no doubt, but the more I tried to perfect it, the more I delayed the launch.

Eventually, one of my team members pulled me aside and said, "We'll never launch this if we keep perfecting it. Sometimes, it's better to take the first step, even if it's not perfect." That conversation became a turning point for me. I had been so consumed by my fear of failure that I had paralyzed myself with perfectionism.

The truth is, you'll never have all the answers, and your work will never be flawless. But that's okay. The power lies in **taking action**, in letting go of perfection, and in moving forward.

4. Creating Space for Growth by Letting Go of Control

The paradox of letting go is that it actually creates more space for growth, not just for yourself but for everyone around you. As I began to trust others and delegate tasks, I discovered that my team could accomplish things I never imagined.

I learned that **delegating is not a sign of weakness; it's a sign of strength**. It shows that you trust the people around you and value their skills and expertise. As a leader, letting go of control allows others to step up and take ownership, which in turn fosters a sense of empowerment, ownership, and pride.

One of the most profound lessons I learned in my career came from reading about **Richard Branson**, the founder of Virgin Group. Branson is known for his emphasis on empowering employees and letting them take ownership of projects. In fact, he's often said:

"The best way of learning about anything is by doing it."

Branson isn't the only one who understands the importance of letting go in leadership. **Jack Welch**, former CEO of General Electric, famously said:

"Before you are a leader, success is all about growing yourself. When you become a leader, success is all about growing others."

This mindset shift was transformational for me. As I started to delegate more tasks, I found that my team not only delivered exceptional work, but they also took initiative in ways that I had never imagined. They brought fresh ideas, new perspectives, and innovative solutions to the table.

By letting go of the need to control every detail, I allowed space for creativity, problem-solving, and innovation to emerge—both in myself and in my team.

5. How to Stop Overthinking and Let the Work Flow

The reality is that **overthinking is a career killer**. It paralyzes decision-making and wastes precious time. I know this because I've been guilty of overthinking every decision, every detail. I've sat at my desk, staring at a proposal or a report, revising it over and over again, even when I knew it was already good enough.

What I learned was that overthinking doesn't lead to better outcomes—it leads to stress and stagnation. When we overthink, we get caught in a cycle of second-guessing and indecision. It's easy to get stuck in that cycle when we're afraid of making mistakes, but in the process, we rob ourselves of opportunities to grow.

In the last few years, I've made a conscious decision to **trust my instincts** and to let go of the need to be perfect in every decision. It's been a game-changer. Now, when I'm faced with a big decision or project, I allow myself to step back, trust my gut, and take action.

Oprah Winfrey, one of the most successful and influential figures in the world, once said:

"You don't become what you want, you become what you believe."

Trusting yourself, trusting your judgment, and letting go of the constant need for validation will open doors you never expected. It's about creating space for intuition and creativity to thrive.

---

6. The Power of Trust: Empowering Your Team

True leadership is about empowering others. It's about letting go of the need to micromanage and instead creating a culture of trust. **Empowering others doesn't just benefit your team—it benefits you**. When you empower others to take ownership and make decisions, it frees you up to focus on the bigger picture and strategic vision.

At first, I was hesitant to delegate. I feared that others wouldn't meet my standards, that they wouldn't do things the way I wanted them to. But as I began to trust my team and give them more responsibility, I saw their skills and strengths shine through. They felt valued and recognized, and the work we accomplished together became stronger and more innovative.

This shift in mindset—from controlling to empowering—was transformative. It's not just about delegation; it's about **creating an environment where people feel valued, trusted, and empowered to contribute.**

Conclusion: Letting Go of Control in Your Career

Letting go of control doesn't mean giving up responsibility or abandoning your goals. It means **shifting your perspective** and recognizing that true growth comes from collaboration, trust, and action. It's about focusing on the bigger picture, empowering others, and embracing imperfection as a part of the process.

As you let go of control in your career, you'll discover new levels of freedom, creativity, and fulfillment. You'll begin to see that success isn't about managing every detail—it's about taking the first step, trusting yourself, and learning to **ride the waves** of uncertainty with confidence.

As you embark on this journey of letting go, remember that you don't have to have it all figured out. You don't need to control everything. **The future belongs to those who trust the process and allow themselves to grow along with the work.**

Chapter 10: Letting Go in Your Relationships

1. Introduction: The Unseen Burden of Trying to Change Others

One of the most common traps we fall into in relationships is the belief that we can—or should—change others. Whether it's a romantic partner, a close friend, or even a family member, we sometimes get caught in the mindset that if someone would just be different, if they would just behave the way we want, things would be better. We pour energy into changing their habits, their opinions, their beliefs—thinking we know best, convinced that **we can fix them**.

But the truth is, trying to change others is a sure path to frustration, disappointment, and emotional exhaustion. It's not only an impossible task—it's also a form of control that ultimately damages relationships. Instead of trying to "fix" others, what if we chose to accept them as they are? What if the key to better relationships was learning how to let go of our need to change others and embrace them, flaws and all?

In my own life, this lesson came with a painful, yet eye-opening experience. I once had a close friend, someone I deeply cared about, but who had a tendency to be negative and cynical. I was constantly trying to help them see the world in a more positive light. I would give advice, point out the silver lining, and encourage them to be more optimistic. And yet, despite all my efforts, nothing changed. The more I tried to "fix" them, the more frustrated I became.

At one point, I realized something profound: **I wasn't actually helping my friend by trying to change them. I was only pushing them away.** They weren't asking for advice, and the truth was, they didn't need me to tell them how to think or feel. What they needed was acceptance, not advice. I needed to let go of my desire to change them, and simply love them for who they were.

It was a turning point in our friendship. I stopped trying to fix them, and instead, I listened more, empathized more, and accepted them more fully. The result? Our relationship deepened. My friend began to open up more, and we were able to build a much healthier, more supportive dynamic.

---

2. How to Stop Trying to Change Others and Accept Them for Who They Are

The desire to change others often comes from a place of love or concern, but more often than not, it's rooted in our own insecurities or frustrations. When we try to change someone, we're essentially saying, **"I don't accept you as you are."** This might be hard to hear, but it's important to recognize that trying to mold people into what we think they should be is a disservice to both them and ourselves.

Acceptance is one of the most powerful tools in any relationship. It's not about resigning yourself to toxic behavior or letting people walk all over you—it's about accepting the reality of who they are, including their flaws, quirks, and imperfections. This acceptance doesn't mean you stop caring or stop trying to help in constructive ways. It simply means that you stop trying to control or manipulate the person into being someone they're not.

One of the best pieces of advice I've ever heard on this topic comes from **Maya Angelou**, who said:

"When someone shows you who they are, believe them the first time."

Angelou's wisdom speaks directly to the heart of acceptance. People show us who they are through their actions, words, and behavior. We can try to rationalize, excuse, or change their behavior all we want, but the truth is in front of us. Accepting people as they are isn't about giving up on them; it's about **seeing them clearly** and respecting them for who they are.

When you stop trying to change someone, you create space for love and connection to flourish. You allow the relationship to breathe, to grow in its own unique way. This doesn't mean you condone harmful behavior or toxic traits, but rather, you stop fighting the fundamental nature of the other person.

3. Building the Best Friendships and Partnerships by Letting Go

Relationships are built on trust, respect, and mutual understanding—not control. The healthiest friendships and romantic partnerships are those where both individuals feel accepted, supported, and free to be themselves without fear of judgment or criticism.

In my personal journey, I've had to learn that relationships thrive not when we try to change each other, but when we allow space for each person to grow into their own best version. I remember a time when I was in a romantic relationship where both of us were constantly trying to change the other. We were young, and our expectations were unrealistic. We both wanted the other person to meet an idealized version of what we thought love should look like.

We argued constantly because of differences in how we handled stress, how we communicated, and how we viewed life. It wasn't until we both stepped back and accepted each other for who we truly were—imperfections and all—that our relationship became more fulfilling. I learned that **acceptance wasn't passive; it was active and empowering**. By letting go of my need to control, I created an environment where both of us could grow, love, and evolve together.

Dr. **John Gottman**, a leading relationship expert, famously says:

"The goal in marriage is not to think alike, but to think together."

This is the essence of any relationship, whether romantic or platonic. Letting go of the need for complete alignment or control allows each person to bring their true selves to the relationship. It's not about forcing agreement—it's about **finding harmony** in the differences.

4. How to Cultivate Healthy, Supportive Relationships Without Feeling Drained

One of the most common pitfalls of relationships is the emotional drain that comes from trying to manage them. When we take on the emotional burdens of others, especially when we try to fix or change them, we risk burning ourselves out. It's easy to become overwhelmed by the needs and problems of the people we care about, especially when we feel responsible for their happiness.

The key to maintaining healthy relationships is to **set boundaries** and to make sure that your needs are being met as well. This is where letting go becomes crucial: you have to let go of the belief that it's your responsibility to manage everyone else's emotional well-being. Relationships, while important, should not come at the cost of your mental health.

In my own life, I've had to learn how to create boundaries in my friendships and family relationships. There was a time when I was emotionally exhausted because I felt I was carrying the weight of everyone else's problems. But over time, I realized that I wasn't being selfish by setting boundaries—I was **preserving my energy** and ensuring that I could show up as my best self.

Brene Brown, an expert on vulnerability and connection, says:

"Daring to set boundaries is about having the courage to love ourselves, even when we risk disappointing others."

Setting boundaries in relationships isn't about being harsh or distant—it's about **creating a foundation of mutual respect**. When you let go of the need to control others and instead focus on what you need, you're empowering both yourself and the people around you. Healthy relationships are those where both individuals can express themselves freely without fear of judgment or manipulation.

A great example of this in practice comes from the story of **Eleanor Roosevelt**, who said:

"No one can make you feel inferior without your consent."

This quote speaks to the power of boundaries and self-respect. When you stop trying to change others, you also stop letting their behavior affect your peace of mind. You build relationships on trust, respect, and **emotional reciprocity**, rather than control.

5. The Art of Letting Go and Trusting in Relationships

Ultimately, letting go in relationships is about **trust**. It's trusting that the people you care about are capable of handling their own lives, their own struggles, and their own growth. It's trusting that the connection you share doesn't need to be forcefully shaped or managed.

I once had a mentor who shared a simple yet profound piece of wisdom with me: "**Let people be who they are. If they love you, they will meet you where you are.**"

This trust—allowing people to come into your life and love you as you are, while also accepting them for who they are—creates a powerful foundation for long-lasting, fulfilling relationships. Trusting someone doesn't mean ignoring their faults or pretending that everything is perfect; it means acknowledging their imperfections and embracing them.

This is where the real magic happens. When you let go of the desire to change others, you open yourself up to deeper, more authentic connections. You allow people the freedom to be themselves, and in doing so, you create space for them to love and support you in return.

6. Conclusion: The Freedom That Comes with Letting Go

Letting go in relationships doesn't mean giving up on people or abandoning them. It means accepting them for who they are and creating space for both of you to grow. It's about trusting that love doesn't need to be forced—it thrives when we allow it to evolve naturally, without trying to control every aspect.

By letting go of the need to change others, you can focus on nurturing the qualities that make your relationships special: trust, respect, empathy, and love. And, just as importantly, you'll experience the freedom of **being loved for exactly who you are**, without the pressure to be perfect.

When you embrace this philosophy in your relationships—whether with friends, family, or romantic partners—you'll find that the connections you share become deeper, more meaningful, and far more fulfilling. By letting go, you create the space for the love, joy, and understanding that you've been seeking all along.

Chapter 11: Letting Go of the Past

Introduction: The Weight of the Past

There's an old saying: **"The past is a foreign country. They do things differently there."** And while it's a clever sentiment, it doesn't capture the full complexity of how the past shapes our present. For many of us, the past is not a foreign country—it is a weight we carry with us everywhere. Whether it's past regrets, guilt, resentment, or memories of loss, the emotional burden of the past can often feel inescapable. These emotions don't just exist as distant memories; they linger, infecting the way we think, the way we behave, and even the way we engage with others.

I know this all too well. I spent years trapped in a cycle of self-criticism, replaying past mistakes in my mind. I held on to guilt from a painful breakup, guilt from decisions I wished I had made differently, and resentment toward people who had wronged me. I thought, **"If I could just go back and fix these things, maybe I would be happy."**

But that mindset kept me stuck. I wanted to move forward, but I couldn't because my mind and heart were still tethered to the past. My healing began the moment I realized that **letting go of the past** wasn't about forgetting it. It was about releasing its hold on me. Once I understood that, my entire life changed.

In this chapter, I'll walk you through the profound act of letting go of the past. How to stop letting regret and resentment define you. How to release guilt. And ultimately, how to forgive—yourself and others—so that you can reclaim your future.

---

1. Freeing Yourself from Regret, Resentment, and Guilt

Regret: The Burden of What Could Have Been

Regret is one of the most paralyzing emotions we can carry. It's the internal dialogue that asks, **"What if?"** We replay the decisions we made in the past over and over again, wondering how different things might have turned out had we made different choices. **Regret is the ghost of "what could have been," and it can trap us in an endless cycle of self-blame.**

I remember a time in my life when I regretted a career decision I made. I had turned down an amazing opportunity to stay in a relationship that I believed was worth sacrificing for. In hindsight, the relationship ended, and the career opportunity was lost forever. For months, I allowed this regret to consume me. I couldn't move forward because I was constantly looking back, asking myself: **"What if I had said yes? What if I hadn't stayed? What if I hadn't played it safe?"**

The late **Dr. Maya Angelou** famously said:

"You did then what you knew how to do, and when you knew better, you did better."

This perspective helped me begin the process of letting go of regret. I realized that at the time, I had made the best decision I could with the knowledge and understanding I had. The key was to **forgive myself** for the decision I had made and to release the belief that I had somehow failed. I had learned from the experience and could move forward better and wiser.

Regret is often tied to the **fear of missed opportunities**, but when we dwell in regret, we miss out on the opportunities of the present. As **Robert Frost** said, "In three words I can sum up everything I've learned about life: it goes on." Life doesn't wait for us to fix the past. It moves forward. And so must we.

Resentment: The Poison We Drink While Waiting for the Other Person to Die

Resentment is another emotion that often holds us back. It's what happens when someone wrongs us, and we can't seem to let go of the anger, hurt, and bitterness. We think that holding onto resentment is somehow a form of justice or revenge, but in reality, it only serves to poison us. **Resentment doesn't hurt the person who wronged us—it only hurts us.**

I used to harbor deep resentment toward a colleague who took credit for my work. At first, I was furious and bitter. I wanted to expose her, to call her out, to make her feel as bad as I did. But the longer I held onto the resentment, the more it weighed on me. I was spending so much of my emotional energy on her actions that I didn't have any left for my own growth. I realized that **resentment was eating me alive**, not her.

As **Nelson Mandela** wisely said:

"Resentment is like drinking poison and then hoping it will kill your enemies."

The truth is, when we hold onto resentment, we become prisoners of the past. We let someone else's actions dictate our emotional well-being. The key to letting go of resentment is forgiveness—not for the other person's sake, but for our own. **Forgiving** doesn't mean condoning the behavior or excusing it; it means choosing not to let the past continue to hold power over you.

Forgiveness is an act of liberation. It's about saying, **"I'm not going to let this event or this person control my happiness anymore."** When I finally forgave my colleague—when I released the resentment—I felt an immense weight lift from my chest. I was free to move forward with my work and my life.

Guilt: The Weight That Keeps Us Stuck in the Past

Guilt is often the most difficult emotion to release. It's tied to our sense of morality and our beliefs about right and wrong. When we feel guilty, we believe we've done something wrong or failed in some way. The problem with guilt, though, is that it has a way of making us believe that we are failures rather than recognizing that we simply made a mistake. Guilt can keep us trapped in a cycle of self-punishment, never allowing us to move forward.

I've spent many nights lying awake, replaying mistakes from my past, thinking, **"I should have known better,"** or **"I should have been more responsible."** But the more I let guilt consume me, the more I realized that I was preventing myself from growing. **Guilt doesn't change the past**, but it can destroy your future if you let it.

The key to releasing guilt is **self-compassion**. We are human, and humans make mistakes. Mistakes do not define us. As **Brené Brown** points out:

"Guilt is I did something bad. Shame is I am bad."

To heal from guilt, we need to separate the action from our identity. We need to **acknowledge the mistake**, learn from it, and then forgive ourselves. **Forgiveness** isn't just for others; it's essential for ourselves. When we forgive ourselves, we release the past and allow ourselves to move forward with grace and compassion.

2. Understanding How Your Past Doesn't Define Your Future

One of the most powerful insights I've learned on this journey is that **your past doesn't define you**. So often, we allow the events of our past to shape our identity and dictate our future. We tell ourselves stories like, **"I'm not good enough because of what happened before,"** or **"I'll never succeed because I failed in the** past." But the truth is, **the past is only one chapter of your story, not the entire book**.

When I was in my early twenties, I believed that I was defined by a bad breakup, a failed job, and the mistakes I made in my personal life. I thought that because I had failed before, I would continue to fail. I felt like the weight of those past experiences would always define who I was. But the turning point came when I realized that I didn't have to carry those labels with me anymore. **I could choose a new story.**

As **Oprah Winfrey** once said:

"You don't become what you want, you become what you believe."

If you believe that your past defines you, then it will. But if you choose to believe that your future is a blank slate, ready for you to write your next chapter, you will unlock an entirely new possibility for your life.

The key to moving forward is to **stop identifying with the past**. The person you were is not the person you are today. And the person you are today is not the person you'll be tomorrow. Each new day is an opportunity to recreate yourself.

3. The Art of Forgiveness and Moving On

The ability to forgive is one of the most powerful tools in letting go of the past. **Forgiveness frees you from the burden of past pain**, and it allows you to move forward with lightness and peace. But forgiveness isn't always easy. It's something that we have to practice—especially when it comes to forgiving ourselves.

There was a time when I felt immense guilt about a mistake I made in a relationship. I had hurt someone I loved deeply, and I couldn't forgive myself for causing them pain. I thought, **"How could I ever make up for this? How could I ever be worthy of love again?"**

But when I finally began to practice **self-forgiveness**, I realized something profound: **Forgiveness is not about erasing the past; it's about making peace with it**. It's about saying, **"I did the best I could at the time, and now I choose to move forward."**

Forgiveness is the key to **reclaiming your future**. It's the way we let go of the past, so that we can open up to the present moment and all the possibilities it holds.

As **Mahatma Gandhi** said:

"The weak can never forgive. Forgiveness is the attribute of the strong."

Forgiveness requires strength—the strength to move on, the strength to release the past, and the strength to create a better future for yourself.

Key Takeaways:

- **Regret** and **resentment** are emotional weights that hold you back. Release them by accepting that you did the best you could at the time and forgiving yourself.

- **Forgiveness** is a gift to yourself. When you forgive others and yourself, you free yourself from the emotional hold the past has over you.

- Your past does not define your future. Every day is a chance to start anew and create the life you want.

- **Self-compassion** is essential for healing. Be kind to yourself, acknowledge your mistakes, and choose to move forward with love and grace.

Letting go of the past isn't about erasing memories or pretending things didn't happen. It's about releasing the emotional grip they have on you, so you can move forward with strength, freedom, and the wisdom of experience.

chapter 12: Letting Go of the Future

Introduction: The Illusion of Control Over the Future

Have you ever found yourself awake at 3 a.m., tossing and turning, consumed by thoughts of the future? Your mind races through a thousand what-ifs: **What if this doesn't work out? What if I fail? What if I'm not ready? What if I miss the opportunity?** The future, with all its uncertainty, often creates a sense of overwhelm. We worry about what's coming, what could go wrong, and how we can possibly prepare for everything that lies ahead.

I have been there. I spent years in a constant cycle of **overthinking** and **worrying** about the future. I'd lay awake at night replaying scenarios in my mind, wondering if I was making the right decisions, wondering if I was doing enough to secure a bright future. The fear of the unknown often paralyzed me from taking the necessary steps forward in my life. I wanted to control everything, make the right choices, and ensure that my future was as perfect as possible.

But the more I tried to control it, the more I realized I was **losing touch with the present**. The future had become an oppressive weight I was carrying around, and it left me feeling anxious, stressed, and disconnected from what mattered most in the moment. **I was chasing a future that wasn't even here yet, and in doing so, I was missing out on the beauty and opportunities of today.**

In this chapter, we will explore how to let go of the future, how to stop overthinking and worrying about what's ahead, and how to trust the process of life unfolding naturally. It's about learning to live in the present while still taking action toward your goals, but without letting fear or anxiety dictate your every move.

---

1. How to Stop Overthinking and Worrying About What's Ahead

Overthinking about the future is a common habit that many people struggle with. We try to anticipate every possible outcome, imagining every scenario, and we often end up feeling paralyzed by the sheer magnitude of our thoughts. But here's the thing: overthinking is not only ineffective, it is also counterproductive. It keeps us stuck in a cycle of **paralysis by analysis**, where we spend so much time planning, analyzing, and strategizing that we fail to take meaningful action.

I remember a time in my life when I was starting a new business venture. I wanted everything to go perfectly, so I spent weeks researching, brainstorming, and worrying about every single aspect. I agonized over marketing strategies, product design, and even how I would handle customer feedback. I even made contingency plans for things that hadn't even happened yet, convinced that the future was something I could control by overanalyzing it. But all this planning didn't help; it only made me more anxious. I was living in a constant state of worry, and as a result, I didn't take the decisive steps I needed to move forward.

This cycle of overthinking and worrying is an illusion of control. The truth is, **the future is inherently uncertain**, and no matter how much we try to predict or plan for it, we can never fully control what's ahead.

As **Eckhart Tolle**, author of *The Power of Now*, writes:

"Realize deeply that the present moment is all you have. Make the Now the primary focus of your life."

The more I embraced the present moment, the less power the future held over me. The more I focused on the actions I could take **today**, the less I found myself trapped in the spiral of what-ifs. **Overthinking doesn't create a better future; it just robs you of the peace and clarity you could be experiencing in the present.**

Breaking the Cycle of Overthinking: A Simple Strategy

The first step to letting go of the future is learning to quiet your mind and **focus on the present moment**. One powerful practice that helped me was **mindfulness**—taking a few moments each day to simply observe my thoughts and feelings without judgment.

Mindfulness isn't about forcing yourself to stop thinking; rather, it's about noticing when your mind starts to wander into future scenarios and gently bringing your attention back to the present moment. You can do this through meditation, breathing exercises, or simply being present with whatever you're doing— whether that's working, talking to a friend, or enjoying a cup of tea.

As **Jon Kabat-Zinn**, the founder of mindfulness-based stress reduction, says:

"You can't stop the waves, but you can learn to surf."

Overthinking is like being caught in the waves of your mind. But by learning to "surf" the thoughts, you can stop being dragged under by them and instead navigate them with ease. This practice won't make your worries disappear entirely, but it will give you the clarity to stop letting them dictate your actions.

2. Trusting the Process: Letting the Future Unfold Naturally

One of the most freeing concepts I have ever learned is that **the future doesn't need to be rushed or forced**. It is easy to get caught up in the idea that we need to constantly be planning, working, and striving for the future. We worry that if we don't do enough, we won't achieve our goals, or that we will somehow "fall behind." But the truth is, **life has its own pace**, and no amount of anxiety can speed it up.

I experienced this firsthand during a period of my life when I was trying to figure out what career path to pursue. I was constantly jumping from one idea to the next, convinced that I needed to know exactly where I was going and how to get there. The pressure to make the "right" decision was overwhelming. But then I realized that by forcing myself to have all the answers, I was actually closing myself off to new possibilities. **I was too busy trying to control the outcome to trust in the natural unfolding of things.**

Trusting the process means understanding that while we can make plans and set goals, we don't need to control every detail. We can take action, make decisions, and put in effort, but we also need to trust that the right opportunities will come at the right time. As **Steve Jobs** famously said:

"You can't connect the dots looking forward; you can only connect them looking backward."

At the time, it seemed like I was wandering aimlessly. But in hindsight, I can see how each step—each misstep, each "wrong" decision—was guiding me toward where I needed to be. **Trusting the process** doesn't mean sitting idly by and waiting for things to happen. It means being present, doing your best in each moment, and trusting that the next step will reveal itself when the time is right.

A simple metaphor I like to use to explain this concept is that of a seed. When you plant a seed, you don't stand over it, watching every second, impatiently waiting for it to grow. You water it, provide it with sunlight, and trust that it will sprout and eventually bloom in its own time. Similarly, you can plant the seeds of your goals and dreams, do the work, and then trust that, over time, they will grow into something beautiful.

---

3. How to Make Decisions from a Place of Calm, Not Fear

One of the most empowering shifts that comes from letting go of the future is learning to make decisions from a place of **calm** and **clarity**, rather than from fear. Too often, we make decisions based on our fears of what could go wrong or our anxieties about what might happen if we choose the wrong path. But fear-driven decisions are rarely the best ones. They often keep us stuck in what's comfortable and familiar, even if it's not what's best for us in the long run.

A few years ago, I was faced with a difficult decision: whether to leave a stable job for an uncertain opportunity. Fear flooded my mind. **What if it didn't work out? What if I failed? What if I couldn't handle the pressure?** I realized that if I allowed those fears to guide my decision, I would likely stay in the same place, stuck in the comfort of the known. So I took a step back. I took a few deep breaths, practiced mindfulness, and listened to my inner voice.

In the end, I made the decision from a place of **calm** and **clarity**, trusting that I had the skills and strength to handle whatever came my way. And that decision changed my life.

Making decisions from a place of calm is not about ignoring your fears, but about acknowledging them and choosing to act despite them. It's about trusting your instincts and knowing that no decision is ever completely risk-free. As **Ralph Waldo Emerson** said:

"Do the thing you fear, and the death of fear is certain."

When we make decisions from a place of **calm and trust**—rather than fear—we open ourselves up to new possibilities. We stop worrying about what could go wrong and start focusing on what could go right.

Key Takeaways

- **Overthinking** the future often leads to paralysis and anxiety. Instead, practice mindfulness and focus on the present moment to quiet the mind.

- **Trust the process**: The future will unfold naturally. By taking action today, you trust that the next step will present itself when the time is right.

- **Make decisions from a place of calm**, not fear. Fear-driven decisions often keep us stuck, but when we act from a place of clarity and trust, we make empowered choices that lead us toward growth and fulfillment.

Conclusion: Embrace the Unknown with Confidence

Letting go of the future is not about abandoning your dreams or goals; it's about giving up the need to control every detail. It's about trusting that the future will unfold as it should, and that you are capable of handling whatever comes your way. Embrace the unknown with confidence, take action in the present, and know that you are already on the right path. The future is waiting for you—don't let fear or worry keep you from stepping into it.

Chapter 13: The Daily Practice of Letting Go

Introduction: Letting Go as a Daily Practice

The journey of letting go doesn't end with a single realization or a one-time decision. It's a lifelong practice, something we need to revisit day after day. The concept of **letting go**—of releasing control, of surrendering the need to manage every detail of our lives—is not something that happens overnight. It's not about a quick fix or a magical solution that will solve all of life's challenges. Instead, it's about developing the habit of letting go.

The daily practice of letting go is about making peace with the inevitable uncertainties of life. It's about learning to step out of the frantic rush to control the future, manage other people's opinions, and hold onto past mistakes. It's about cultivating inner peace and balance in a world that often feels chaotic and overwhelming.

In this chapter, we will explore how to **cultivate the habit of letting go every day**, how to incorporate simple mindfulness techniques into your routine to stay present, and how to create rituals that help you focus on what you can control.

1. How to Cultivate the Habit of Letting Go Every Day

Letting go is not something you do once and then forget about. It's something you **practice**—every single day. In the same way that we build physical strength through regular exercise, we cultivate mental and emotional strength through daily practice.

I remember a time in my life when I was going through a particularly difficult period. I felt overwhelmed by responsibilities, anxious about the future, and weighed down by past regrets. No matter how hard I tried to manage everything, I just couldn't shake the feeling that I was losing control.

One evening, as I was sitting alone in my room, I had a moment of clarity. I realized that I didn't need to **control everything**—I needed to **let go** of the idea that I could manage all aspects of my life. I began practicing the art of letting go in small moments throughout the day. It started with something as simple as letting go of the need to have a perfectly organized schedule. I learned to trust that things would fall into place, even if I didn't have everything planned to the letter.

From that moment forward, I committed myself to cultivating the habit of letting go. I began incorporating mindfulness and other practices into my daily routine to help me detach from the anxiety of trying to control every detail.

Here are a few ways to cultivate the habit of letting go:

Start with Your Breath

One of the simplest, yet most powerful, ways to let go of stress and anxiety is by focusing on your breath. Breathing is something we do automatically, but when we consciously pay attention to our breath, we can shift our focus from the chaos in our minds to the calm in our bodies.

The practice of deep breathing is an easy and accessible way to ground yourself in the present moment. Whenever I felt overwhelmed or anxious, I would stop and take five deep, intentional breaths. This small act of mindfulness would instantly calm my nervous system and help me let go of the tension I was carrying.

Breathing is your anchor in the present moment— whenever you feel yourself slipping into worry or overthinking, return to your breath.

As **Thich Nhat Hanh**, the renowned Zen master, said:

"Feelings come and go like clouds in a windy sky. Conscious breathing is my anchor."

Let Go of Perfectionism

One of the biggest barriers to letting go is the pressure to be perfect. Perfectionism often keeps us trapped in a cycle of constant striving and self-criticism. We fear making mistakes, so we try to control everything down to the smallest detail. But perfection is an illusion. The pursuit of perfection keeps us from experiencing the beauty of imperfection.

I once worked with a client who was a **perfectionist** in every area of her life. She would spend hours tweaking and refining her work, constantly chasing a version of success that didn't exist. I encouraged her to embrace the idea of "good enough" rather than "perfect." The moment she let go of the need to be perfect, she experienced a profound shift in her mindset. She found more joy in her work and was able to complete tasks more efficiently because she no longer agonized over every detail.

Perfectionism is a trap. Letting go of the need to be perfect allows you to experience life more fully, without the constant pressure to meet impossible standards.

---

2. Simple Mindfulness Techniques to Stay Present and Peaceful

Mindfulness is the practice of being fully present and aware of your thoughts, feelings, and surroundings without judgment. It is one of the most effective tools for letting go. Mindfulness helps you become aware of when you're holding onto something—whether it's a fear of the future, a resentment from the past, or an urge to control someone or something—and it allows you to gently release it.

Mindfulness Through Meditation

Meditation is one of the most well-known mindfulness practices. It's a simple way to train your mind to stay present and to let go of distracting thoughts. I started meditating daily after a particularly stressful period in my life. I was dealing with constant pressure at work and personal challenges, and I felt as though my mind was racing at all times.

I began with just five minutes a day, sitting quietly and focusing on my breath. Over time, I found that meditation helped me detach from my anxious thoughts and quiet the constant mental chatter. It was in these moments of stillness that I began to truly understand the value of letting go.

As **Jon Kabat-Zinn**, the creator of mindfulness-based stress reduction, says:

"You can't stop the waves, but you can learn to surf."

Meditation teaches you to let go of the need to control your thoughts and emotions. Instead, you simply observe them without attachment and allow them to pass naturally.

Mindful Awareness in Daily Activities

Mindfulness doesn't have to be limited to formal meditation. You can practice mindfulness throughout your day, whether you're eating, walking, or even washing dishes. The key is to be fully engaged in the present moment, rather than allowing your mind to wander to past regrets or future worries.

One of my favorite mindfulness practices is mindful walking. Whenever I feel overwhelmed or scattered, I step outside and take a slow, deliberate walk. I focus on the sensation of my feet touching the ground, the sound of my breath, and the sights and sounds around me.

This simple practice of mindful walking grounds me and helps me reset my mental state.

As **Ram Dass**, the spiritual teacher, once said:

"Be here now."

Practicing mindfulness helps you release the need to constantly plan or worry about the future. It's about accepting each moment as it comes and trusting that you are exactly where you need to be.

---

3. Creating Rituals That Keep You Focused on What You Can Control

Another key to the daily practice of letting go is creating rituals that help you stay focused on what you can control. Rituals provide structure and stability in your day and help you stay anchored in the present moment. These rituals are a way of prioritizing what truly matters, while letting go of the things that don't serve you.

Morning Rituals to Start Your Day with Intention

I found that starting my day with a simple morning ritual set the tone for the rest of my day. Whether it was a few minutes of meditation, a cup of coffee while reading a few pages of a book, or a short walk outside, I made sure to start my day grounded in the present moment.

Morning rituals help you reclaim your power before the demands of the day take over. By setting a positive, intentional tone in the morning, you are more likely to stay centered and less likely to be swept up in the chaos of the day.

One of my favorite quotes by **Benjamin Franklin** sums up the importance of morning rituals:

"Early to bed and early to rise makes a man healthy, wealthy, and wise."

Evening Rituals to Let Go of the Day

Just as morning rituals help you set a positive tone for the day, evening rituals help you let go of the day's stresses and prepare for a restful night's sleep. At the end of each day, I practice a brief **reflection ritual**. I review the day, acknowledging what went well and what didn't, and then I let go of any lingering stress or worries.

I also practice **journaling** as part of my evening ritual. Writing about the day allows me to release any emotional tension I may be holding onto. It's a powerful way to reflect, learn, and let go of whatever no longer serves me.

As **Maya Angelou** said:

"We delight in the beauty of the butterfly, but rarely admit the changes it has gone through to achieve that beauty."

Journaling is a way to reflect on your own transformation—acknowledging the changes you've gone through and letting go of the weight of the day.

Key Takeaways

- The **habit of letting go** must be cultivated daily. It is a practice, not a one-time event.

- **Mindfulness**—whether through meditation or in daily activities—helps you stay grounded in the present moment and release the need to control.

- Creating **rituals**—both in the morning and evening—helps you focus on what you can control, setting a positive tone for the day and releasing stress at night.

- Letting go is a process, but with consistent practice, it becomes a natural and powerful part of your life.

Conclusion: Embracing the Daily Practice

The practice of letting go is not just a theory or a concept—it is a way of life. By cultivating the habit of letting go every day, you can create more space for peace, joy, and fulfillment. It allows you to live with greater intention and less stress, to embrace the present moment, and to trust that you are exactly where you need to be.

Remember: letting go isn't about giving up; it's about freeing yourself from the burden of trying to control everything. It's about trusting in the process and knowing that you are already enough. Let go of the need to manage every detail, and watch as your life unfolds with greater ease, clarity, and purpose.

The daily practice of letting go is the key to living a life of freedom and peace. Embrace it, and watch your life transform.

Chapter 14: The Ripple Effect: How Letting Go Transforms Your Entire Life

Introduction: The Ripple Effect of Letting Go

When you let go of something, you may feel as if you are relinquishing control, but what you are actually doing is freeing yourself to embrace a life of greater ease, peace, and authenticity. The act of "letting go" is like tossing a pebble into a pond—the impact ripples outward, affecting not only the immediate area but also the wider environment. This ripple effect is not just an abstract metaphor; it's a profound and tangible shift that can transform the way you experience every aspect of your life.

In this chapter, we will explore how a **single shift in mindset**—the decision to let go—creates a chain of positive changes in your life. We'll dive into real-life stories of people who have used the "Let Them" mindset to radically change their lives, and examine how letting go of what no longer serves you enhances your **health, wealth, and happiness.**

1. How One Shift in Mindset Creates a Ripple of Positive Change

For years, I was caught in a cycle of trying to control everything around me. I obsessed over the smallest details in my work, relationships, and personal life. I believed that if I could just manage everything perfectly, I would be happy. But the more I tried to control, the more I felt overwhelmed and out of balance.

It wasn't until I realized the power of **letting go** that everything began to shift. The moment I made the conscious decision to stop trying to manage every aspect of my life was the moment everything changed for the better. At first, it felt like a huge leap of faith. Letting go of control felt terrifying. What would happen if I stopped worrying about how things would unfold? What if things went wrong?

But as I began to let go of the need to micromanage every detail, I experienced something remarkable: **space**. Space to breathe, space to think, and space to allow things to unfold naturally. And in that space, something profound happened: **opportunity**. I began to notice possibilities I hadn't seen before. My relationships became richer. My work became more focused and impactful. I found myself moving forward with greater ease and confidence.

As **Tony Robbins** wisely said:

"The only limit to your impact is your imagination and commitment."

In letting go, I unlocked a world of potential I hadn't even known existed.

Letting go isn't about giving up—it's about creating the conditions for **growth**. Once you stop clinging to control, you allow life to flow freely, and the opportunities that emerge are often far more beautiful and fulfilling than anything you could have planned.

---

2. Real-Life Stories of People Who've Transformed Their Lives with "Let Them"

Alicia's Journey: From Burnout to Freedom

Alicia, a successful executive, had spent years climbing the corporate ladder. She was always the one who took on extra projects, stayed late at the office, and ensured that everything was "perfect." She prided herself on being in control, but this came at a personal cost. Alicia was burned out, disconnected from her family, and struggling with anxiety.

One day, she came across a podcast where the host spoke about the **"Let Them"** philosophy—the power of releasing control and trusting others. Alicia was skeptical at first. "What if things fall apart?" she thought. But something inside her knew that if she didn't make a change, she would keep spiraling into burnout.

Alicia took the plunge. She started by delegating more tasks at work, trusting her team members to handle responsibilities without constant oversight. At home, she began to let go of the unrealistic standards she had set for herself as a mother and wife. Instead of trying to do everything perfectly, she started allowing space for spontaneity and imperfection.

The results were nothing short of miraculous. Alicia's stress levels dropped, her relationships deepened, and her productivity at work actually improved. By letting go, she stopped burning herself out and began to thrive in all areas of her life.

Alicia's story is a testament to the fact that **letting go** doesn't mean giving up—it means giving yourself permission to experience life with greater joy, freedom, and fulfillment.

Mark's Transformation: From Self-Doubt to Success

Mark, an aspiring entrepreneur, was stuck in a loop of self-doubt. He constantly compared himself to other successful business owners and felt that he would never measure up. He was always looking for the "perfect" business idea, the "perfect" team, and the "perfect" execution plan. But the more he tried to control every variable, the more overwhelmed he became. His business never took off because he was paralyzed by his need for perfection.

One day, Mark had a breakthrough. After listening to a talk on the power of **letting go**, he decided to take a different approach. Instead of worrying about every small detail, Mark focused on taking action. He let go of the idea that everything had to be perfect. He started small, launched his business with a simple plan, and learned as he went along.

Today, Mark is the proud owner of a thriving business. His company is growing, his confidence has skyrocketed, and most importantly, he no longer feels consumed by fear and doubt. **Letting go of the need for control** was the key to his success. As **Albert Einstein** once said:

"The definition of insanity is doing the same thing over and over again and expecting different results."

By letting go, Mark stepped into the success he had been chasing for years.

---

3. How Letting Go Enhances Your Health, Wealth, and Happiness

Health: Letting Go of Stress and Tension

The impact of letting go is perhaps most immediately felt in your health. When you constantly try to control every detail of your life, stress levels rise, and your body can become overwhelmed. The cycle of worry, overthinking, and fear triggers a constant fight-or-flight response, putting strain on your nervous system and weakening your immune system.

When you practice **letting go**, your body experiences a profound shift. You move out of the stress response and into a state of relaxation and calm. Studies have shown that reducing stress can lower your risk of heart disease, improve digestion, and even extend your lifespan.

A personal story illustrates this point: I once worked with a woman named Sarah, who had been dealing with chronic headaches and fatigue for years. Her doctors couldn't pinpoint the cause, but after several sessions of stress management and practicing **letting go**, Sarah realized her constant worry and need to control her life were causing her physical symptoms.

She began practicing daily relaxation techniques, including deep breathing, meditation, and journaling, to release the tension she had been holding onto. Within a few weeks, her headaches diminished, and her energy returned. By **letting go**, Sarah not only improved her mental health but also experienced significant physical healing.

Wealth: Letting Go of Scarcity Mindset

The mindset of scarcity is another powerful barrier that prevents many people from experiencing abundance. When we hold onto the belief that there is never enough—whether it's money, success, or opportunity—we feel trapped in a cycle of fear and lack. We grasp at opportunities and try to control our financial futures, only to find ourselves exhausted and frustrated.

The key to unlocking true wealth is shifting from a **scarcity mindset** to an **abundance mindset**. By letting go of the fear of losing what we have, we open ourselves up to receiving more. This doesn't mean sitting back and waiting for money to magically appear; it means trusting that the universe has an abundance of opportunities, and by letting go of control, you create space for those opportunities to manifest.

Take the example of **John**, an entrepreneur who had spent years working in a job that left him feeling unfulfilled and financially strapped. He was always focused on controlling every aspect of his income, but he found that the more he clung to his financial fears, the less money he seemed to attract. Once he let go of the idea that he needed to "hustle harder" or "chase success," he opened himself to new opportunities.

By taking a step back and allowing things to unfold naturally, John found new revenue streams, expanded his business, and achieved financial freedom. As **Oprah Winfrey** wisely states:

"The more you praise and celebrate your life, the more there is in life to celebrate."

By letting go of control and trusting the process, John's wealth grew not only in monetary terms but in the richness of his life experiences.

Happiness: Letting Go of Expectations

One of the most profound changes that letting go brings is a deep sense of **happiness**. So often, our happiness is tied to expectations—of how our lives should look, how others should behave, or how much we should have achieved by a certain age. These expectations create a constant cycle of dissatisfaction because life rarely meets the ideals we set.

Letting go of these expectations allows you to experience happiness in the present moment, without needing everything to be perfect. It allows you to accept life as it is, appreciating the beauty in the journey rather than fixating on a specific destination.

A woman named **Linda** shared with me that she had spent years chasing happiness by setting rigid goals and expectations for herself. Once she decided to let go of those expectations and embrace life as it came, she discovered a new, deep sense of happiness. She began to find joy in the everyday moments—spending time with her family, enjoying her hobbies, and savoring simple pleasures.

Linda's story exemplifies what **Eckhart Tolle** meant when he said:

"Realize deeply that the present moment is all you ever have."

When you let go of the need to control everything, you open the door to greater joy, peace, and fulfillment.

Conclusion: The Ripple Effect in Action

Letting go is not a one-time decision—it's a **continuous practice** that ripples outward into every corner of your life. It's a mindset shift that begins with small moments of release, but over time, it transforms the way you live, work, and interact with others.

The ripple effect of letting go impacts your health, wealth, and happiness. By releasing your grip on what you cannot control, you create more space for the things that matter most. You become more peaceful, more present, and more aligned with the life you were meant to lead.

As you embrace the "Let Them" mindset, you'll notice a transformation unfolding in your life. Every time you let go, you unlock a new level of freedom, clarity, and opportunity. The ripple effect is real, and it has the power to change your life for the better—one moment at a time.

Chapter 15: The Freedom to Live Your Life on Your Own Terms

Introduction: The Ultimate Freedom

What if you could live your life completely on your own terms? What if you didn't have to meet other people's expectations or live by a set of rigid rules that aren't even yours? What if, instead of living for others, you lived for yourself, aligning your daily choices with your true desires, values, and passions? This chapter is all about **the freedom** to do just that: to **define success and happiness for yourself**, to **embrace the life you've always wanted**, and to realize the ultimate freedom of living a life without limits.

For much of my life, I was living according to other people's definitions of success. I had a clear vision of what I thought I *should* be doing, based on society's standards, family expectations, and the opinions of those around me. I followed the well-trodden path that I was told would lead to happiness—finish school, get a good job, climb the career ladder, marry, have kids, and retire comfortably. Yet, despite checking all these boxes, I often felt **unfulfilled** and **disconnected** from my true self. There was always this underlying feeling that I was chasing someone else's dream, not my own.

It wasn't until I started practicing the art of **letting go** that things began to change. Letting go of what I thought I "should" do and embracing what I truly **wanted** to do brought me a level of peace and freedom I had never known before. This chapter is about helping you achieve the same level of freedom by **defining your own success** and **living life without limits**.

---

1. Defining Success and Happiness for Yourself

We are often taught that success is defined by external markers: wealth, status, achievements, and the validation of others. Society, our families, and even our friends often have a strong influence on what we perceive success to be. But if you've ever reached one of those "success milestones" only to find that it didn't bring you the happiness you expected, then you know that the traditional definition of success is incomplete.

I'll share a personal story that illustrates this point. In my early 30s, I achieved what many people would consider "success." I had a well-paying job, a nice apartment, a comfortable life, and was surrounded by friends and family. Yet, deep down, I felt **empty**. Despite all the accomplishments, I couldn't shake the feeling that I was living someone else's life. It wasn't that I didn't appreciate what I had—it was that I was disconnected from my true desires.

One day, a friend of mine, who had recently made a huge career change, sat me down and asked, "Are you happy with what you're doing?" I remember feeling a twinge of guilt, as if admitting I wasn't fulfilled was somehow disrespectful to all the sacrifices I had made. But I had to be honest. "No," I said. "I'm not sure this is *my* path."

That conversation was the spark that began my journey of **redefining success**. I had spent so much time striving for what society said was important that I had lost sight of what was important to **me**. I needed to reflect on what made my heart beat faster, what made me feel truly alive. I needed to define my own version of success.

The first step was **disconnecting** from the societal benchmarks I had internalized and examining what truly mattered to me: personal growth, creativity, meaningful connections, and contributing to others' lives in a positive way. **Success**, for me, began to mean something different. It wasn't about climbing the corporate ladder or accumulating material wealth; it was about living authentically, aligning my actions with my values, and finding joy in the process rather than fixating on a destination.

Steve Jobs once said:

"Your work is going to fill a large part of your life, and the only way to be truly satisfied is to do what you believe is great work. And the only way to do great work is to love what you do."

Letting go of external expectations allowed me to embrace a life I could truly love, one that was built on my terms.

---

2. Embracing the Life You've Always Wanted by Letting Go of What No Longer Serves You

Letting go is often a **difficult and painful** process, especially when it involves releasing what has been part of your life for a long time. You may have spent years chasing a career, a relationship, or a goal that once seemed important, only to realize that it no longer serves you. But this is the **paradox of letting go**: while it may feel like you're losing something, what you are really doing is **creating space** for something far more meaningful and aligned with your true self.

I remember when I made the decision to walk away from a job I had been in for over a decade. On the surface, it seemed like the ideal career—great pay, prestigious title, benefits—but inside, I felt trapped. My creativity was stifled, and I felt increasingly disillusioned. Yet, leaving this stable job felt like **shedding an old skin**, one that I had clung to for security.

It was hard. I had invested so much time and energy into my career, and letting go felt like a huge leap of faith. What if I failed? What if I disappointed everyone around me? But once I let go of the fear of failure and embraced the unknown, my life opened up in ways I never imagined. I finally had the freedom to pursue my passions, to explore new opportunities, and to create a life that felt right for me.

The key here is that **letting go of what no longer serves you** doesn't mean giving up—it means making a conscious choice to prioritize your well-being, your growth, and your happiness. It means letting go of relationships, habits, or goals that have become burdens rather than sources of joy. It's a powerful act of self-love and self-respect.

Maya Angelou once wisely said:

"You may not control all the events that happen to you, but you can decide not to be reduced by them."

By letting go, you begin to reclaim your power and design the life you've always wanted.

---

3. The Ultimate Freedom: Living a Life Without Limits

Living without limits means stepping outside the box of societal norms and expectations. It's about realizing that the only limits that exist are the ones we place on ourselves. When we let go of the fear of judgment, the fear of failure, and the fear of the unknown, we open the door to a life of limitless possibilities.

One of the most profound shifts that comes from letting go is the ability to **create your own path**. When I started my journey of embracing my authentic self, I quickly realized that the "rules" I had been following no longer applied. There was no one right way to live, no one perfect path to follow. The freedom to live without limits meant allowing myself to explore new possibilities, to try things I had never imagined, and to make mistakes without fear of failure.

Richard Branson, the entrepreneur and founder of Virgin Group, once said:

"You don't learn to walk by following rules. You learn by doing, and by falling over."

Letting go of perfectionism, control, and expectations freed me to try new things, take risks, and embrace the unexpected. It wasn't about getting everything "right" or following a set formula; it was about living in a way that felt true to who I was and what I wanted.

This sense of freedom can also be seen in **Kristen's story**. Kristen had spent years working in a high-paying but soul-draining job. Like many people, she had been taught that a successful career and financial stability were the ultimate indicators of a meaningful life. However, after a life-altering health scare, she began to question everything. She realized that the life she was living was not the life she wanted.

Kristen decided to **let go** of her corporate career and pursue her passion for art. It wasn't an easy decision— there were a lot of doubts and fears—but the freedom she found in following her heart was immeasurable.

Today, she's a thriving artist who has found not only **financial success** but also **personal fulfillment**.

When we release our fears and limitations, we make room for the life we've always wanted. Living without limits means embracing the unknown, trusting the journey, and having faith that the universe will guide us toward the right opportunities. As **Nelson Mandela** famously said:

"There is nothing like returning to a place that remains unchanged to find the ways in which you yourself have altered."

---

4. Realizing the Life You Truly Want

The freedom to live your life on your own terms is one of the most powerful gifts you can give yourself. It requires **bravery**, **self-awareness**, and a willingness to let go of the things that are no longer serving you. But the payoff is immense. When you stop living according to the expectations of others and start aligning with your true desires, you create a life that is rich in purpose, joy, and fulfillment.

I often think back to the time when I decided to finally **let go** and live life on my terms. It wasn't a one-time decision—it was a series of small, courageous steps. And every time I let go, I moved closer to the life I was always meant to live.

The freedom to live without limits is about realizing that you are worthy of living a life that lights you up, that excites you, and that brings you deep, lasting happiness. By defining your own success, embracing what truly matters to you, and letting go of the past, you give yourself permission to **live fully**.

Life is waiting for you—waiting for you to release your grip on the things that are holding you back, to shed the layers that don't belong, and to step into the future with confidence and joy. This is the ultimate freedom: to live the life you choose, not the life you're told to live.

Conclusion: Living Life on Your Own Terms

Living life on your own terms is not only possible—it's your birthright. By embracing the principles of letting go, you can redefine success, happiness, and freedom in a way that aligns with who you truly are. You don't have to live according to anyone else's blueprint for life. When you let go of expectations, fear, and limitations, you create a path that is uniquely yours. And in doing so, you unlock the ultimate freedom: the freedom to live fully, authentically, and joyfully.

The life you've always wanted is waiting for you. It begins with one simple step: **let go of what no longer serves you** and trust that the best is yet to come.

Chapter 16: Letting Go of the Need to Control Everything

Introduction: The Illusion of Control

Control is an illusion. It's one of the most pervasive myths we tell ourselves—this idea that we can somehow, by sheer will or effort, control everything around us. If we could just manage the details, micromanage our environment, or make everything go according to plan, life would be perfect, right? But in reality, this obsession with control is not only exhausting, it's **counterproductive**. When we try to control everything, we inadvertently create resistance, stress, and anxiety.

In this chapter, we will explore how letting go of the need to control can create a profound shift in your life. It's not about giving up your goals or aspirations; rather, it's about **trusting the process** and **accepting the uncertainty** that comes with being human. The freedom that comes from releasing the need for control allows you to flow with life, embrace new opportunities, and cultivate deeper peace within yourself.

1. The Paradox of Control: The More We Try to Hold On, the More We Lose

I've been guilty of trying to control every aspect of my life, and I know I'm not alone in this. I remember in my early years of adulthood, I was a **perfectionist**—always striving to have everything just right. From the smallest details of my appearance to the biggest aspects of my career, I tried to control every element of my existence. The fear of letting go and trusting life to unfold led to feelings of constant **tension** and **exhaustion**.

When you believe that **control** is the key to a successful and peaceful life, you create a **trap** for yourself. You are constantly managing expectations, worrying about the future, and forcing things to happen instead of allowing them to unfold naturally. As a result, the more you try to hold on to control, the more you lose. Life becomes a constant battle, one where you rarely feel at ease.

Eckhart Tolle, in his book *The Power of Now*, says:

"The more you try to control something, the more you are bound to suffer."

This became painfully clear to me in a moment that stands out in my memory. I was working on a big project at work, one that I thought would be the key to my promotion. I spent hours obsessing over every detail, micromanaging every decision, and creating pressure where none was needed. When things didn't go as planned, I spiraled into frustration and burnout.

It wasn't until I realized that I was **gripping too tightly** that I began to let go. The moment I stopped forcing the outcome and allowed the project to flow naturally, everything started to fall into place. The project turned out better than I could have imagined, and I found that, in the end, my success didn't depend on controlling every aspect, but rather on trusting myself and the process.

2. Letting Go of the Need for Approval

One of the most common ways we attempt to control our lives is by seeking **validation** and **approval** from others. Whether it's from our family, friends, colleagues, or even strangers on social media, we often find ourselves constantly seeking reassurance that we are doing things "right." This need for approval can be paralyzing, as it keeps us stuck in a cycle of **people-pleasing** and self-doubt.

I was no stranger to this pattern. Early in my career, I had an overwhelming need to be liked by everyone. I would go out of my way to meet others' expectations, even if it meant compromising my own values. In the process, I lost sight of who I truly was and what I really wanted out of life. I was constantly adjusting my behavior to fit others' ideals, and I felt drained and unfulfilled.

Brené Brown, a research professor and author on vulnerability, talks about how **shame** and **fear of disapproval** can prevent us from living authentically:

"The opposite of belonging is fitting in. Belonging doesn't require us to change who we are; it requires us to be who we are."

When I finally realized that I didn't need anyone's approval to be worthy of success and happiness, everything changed. I began to trust myself more, make decisions based on what felt right for me, and let go of the need to control how others perceived me. That's when I started feeling true **freedom**.

---

3. Embracing Life's Uncertainty

Life is inherently uncertain. Despite our best efforts to plan, organize, and predict, there are no guarantees. And that's okay. In fact, it's more than okay—it's **liberating**. Once we let go of the need for control, we open ourselves up to the unexpected **magic** of life. It's in the uncertainty that we find the opportunity to grow, learn, and transform.

In my own life, the most significant moments of growth have come during times of uncertainty. There was a time when I was uncertain about my career path, wondering if I should stay in a job that no longer fulfilled me. Instead of continuing to try to control the outcome and fight against my inner conflict, I decided to embrace the uncertainty and explore new possibilities.

It was in this space of not knowing what would happen next that I found the courage to take risks, pursue my passions, and ultimately create a career that aligned with my true self.

Rainer Maria Rilke, the renowned poet, captured this beautifully when he said:

"Be patient toward all that is unsolved in your heart and try to love the questions themselves."

By letting go of the need for certainty, we give ourselves permission to **trust the process**, knowing that the answers will come when the time is right.

---

4. The Freedom of Letting Go of Control

When you stop trying to control every aspect of your life, you will experience a profound shift. You'll feel more **relaxed**, more **present**, and more at peace with yourself and the world around you. The simple act of **letting go** is one of the most powerful tools you have for creating a life that is meaningful, joyful, and fulfilling.

By embracing uncertainty, releasing your grip on external validation, and trusting the flow of life, you open yourself up to the richness of the present moment. You will no longer be burdened by the weight of control; instead, you will be free to live fully in each moment, knowing that the path forward is exactly as it needs to be.

As **Deepak Chopra** wisely said:

"The more you let go, the more life flows."

Conclusion: The Freedom in Letting Go of Control

Letting go of the need to control everything is not about surrendering to chaos or giving up on your goals; it's about releasing the tension that comes from believing you can control outcomes that are outside of your hands. When you trust in the process, you invite **flow**, **creativity**, and **peace** into your life. The more you embrace uncertainty, the more you will experience the freedom to live authentically and purposefully. In the end, the key to true happiness and fulfillment is not in controlling everything around us, but in learning to trust life as it unfolds.

Chapter 17: Letting Go of the "Shoulds"

Introduction: Breaking Free from "Should"

How many times have you told yourself, "I **should** be doing this" or "I **shouldn't** be feeling this way"? The word "should" is one of the most insidious mental traps we fall into. It's the voice of **societal expectations**, **family pressure**, and even our own inner critic. "Should" creates an image of how things are **supposed** to be and sets unrealistic standards that keep us stuck in cycles of guilt, shame, and frustration.

In this chapter, we'll explore how **letting go of the "shoulds"** can set you free to live authentically and pursue a life that is in alignment with your true desires. This is a powerful practice that requires awareness, self-compassion, and a willingness to break free from the **burden** of expectations that don't serve you.

1. The Weight of the "Shoulds"

For much of my life, I lived in a constant state of "should." I should be more successful. I should be more confident. I should be doing more with my time. I should be a better friend, partner, and professional. The list was endless. The problem with these "shoulds" is that they create a version of ourselves that is constantly **chasing an ideal** that doesn't exist. Instead of being present with who we are, we focus on who we think we should be.

I remember a time when I was so consumed with the idea of "should" that I became **paralyzed** by indecision. I couldn't make a move without wondering if it was what I was "supposed" to do. Should I take this job? Should I stay in this relationship? Should I be more ambitious?

One day, I realized that the word "should" was controlling my life. It was dictating my choices and preventing me from living authentically. I decided that I would start questioning the **"shoulds"** in my life and challenge them.

---

2. Letting Go of the "Shoulds" of Perfectionism

The "shoulds" are often deeply tied to perfectionism— the belief that you must be perfect to be **worthy**. The problem with perfectionism is that it sets you up for failure because perfection doesn't exist. It's an unattainable standard that only leads to **self-criticism**, **burnout**, and frustration.

Elizabeth Gilbert, author of *Eat Pray Love*, talks about the **freedom** that comes when we let go of perfection:

"Perfectionism is just fear in fancy shoes. It's the voice of the oppressor."

In my own life, letting go of perfectionism meant releasing the grip on these **unrealistic standards** I had set for myself. I started accepting myself for who I was, flaws and all. This shift in mindset allowed me to feel more **peaceful**, **creative**, and **fulfilled**.

---

3. Breaking Free from Society's Expectations

Society tells us what we should be, how we should look, what we should have achieved by a certain age. But when we live by these external standards, we deny our own uniqueness and rob ourselves of the chance to live our true, **authentic** lives.

I remember a moment when I stopped caring about living up to society's timeline. I was in my 30s and hadn't followed the traditional path to career success. Instead of feeling shame or guilt, I embraced my own **journey** and began creating the life that worked for me, not the life that was expected of me.

---

4. Creating Your Own "Should-Free" Life

Letting go of the "shoulds" is about recognizing that you are enough exactly as you are. It's about **choosing** what feels right for you, regardless of external opinions or societal pressures. When you stop measuring your life against someone else's standards, you make room for the freedom to be truly yourself.

Conclusion: The Power of Living Without "Shoulds"

Letting go of the "shoulds" gives you the freedom to live in alignment with your **true self**. You no longer feel trapped by the weight of expectations, guilt, or shame. Instead, you embrace the present moment and make choices based on what truly matters to you.

By letting go of the "shoulds," you unlock the power to live authentically and with purpose, unburdened by the expectations that once held you back. This is where true freedom begins.

Ending: Embracing the Freedom to Let Go

As we come to the end of this journey, it's important to take a moment and reflect on what you've learned and what lies ahead. The **Let Them Theory** is not just a concept or a tool—it's a **way of life**. It's about finding peace in the midst of chaos, embracing the ebb and flow of life, and reclaiming your personal power by **letting go** of what no longer serves you. The true magic of this mindset comes from trusting the process, believing in yourself, and releasing the grip on control that often holds us back.

Remember that **letting go** doesn't mean giving up—it means **letting life unfold** in its own beautiful way. It means freeing yourself from the unnecessary burdens of other people's expectations, self-doubt, fear, and regret. It means breaking free from the constant pressure to **be perfect**, the need for approval, and the temptation to compare yourself to others. Letting go means standing in your truth, trusting your instincts, and embracing your own unique path to success and happiness.

Over the course of this book, you've learned how to **reclaim your personal power**, build unshakable confidence, and cultivate deep, meaningful relationships. You've discovered the **freedom** that comes when you stop wasting energy on things you can't control and focus instead on the areas of your life that matter most. Whether it's **career success**, personal relationships, emotional health, or simply living with greater peace and joy, the Let Them Theory empowers you to let go of the distractions and chaos that once consumed you and focus on what truly matters: YOU.

The Power of Choice

As you move forward, understand that **letting go** is not a one-time event—it's a continual practice. You will encounter moments where you feel the urge to grip tightly to old patterns, fears, or judgments. But remember, every time you choose to **let go** of what's holding you back, you create **space for something better**. Every decision to release control, fear, or doubt opens the door to new possibilities, new growth, and new levels of happiness.

You hold the power to change your life simply by shifting your mindset. It's all about making the choice to embrace freedom and joy, rather than clinging to the constraints of **shoulds**, **perfectionism**, or **external validation**. As **Maya Angelou** so beautifully put it:

"We delight in the beauty of the butterfly, but rarely admit the changes it has gone through to achieve that beauty."

Just like the butterfly, your journey through the Let Them Theory will require change. You may not see the transformation overnight, but the more you let go, the more you'll witness the beauty of your own evolution.

The Ripple Effect of Letting Go

Letting go doesn't just change your own life—it creates a **ripple effect** that impacts everyone around you. The energy you bring into your relationships, your career, and your personal life is contagious. When you stop fighting, comparing, and controlling, you begin to influence the people around you in ways that are subtle but powerful. Your ability to release judgment, negativity, and fear inspires others to do the same.

Think about the people in your life. When you allow them to be who they are, without the need to control or fix them, you create **space** for them to thrive. When you stop seeking approval and start living authentically, you give others the permission to do the same. This mutual exchange of freedom and acceptance strengthens relationships and fosters **genuine connection**.

One of the most powerful aspects of the Let Them Theory is that by **letting go**, you encourage the people around you to let go as well. The more you practice these principles in your life, the more you inspire others to do the same. It's a beautiful cycle of growth and liberation.

A Life Without Limits

The ultimate promise of the Let Them Theory is that you have the power to create a life **without limits**. By releasing your attachment to outcomes, expectations, and control, you open yourself up to new possibilities—both for your **personal growth** and for the **impact** you can make in the world. There are no limits to what you can achieve when you stop holding yourself back with unnecessary restrictions.

The life you desire—full of joy, peace, success, and meaningful connection—is waiting for you on the other side of **letting go**. The key is to trust in the process, to **embrace uncertainty**, and to remember that the only thing you truly control is your **reaction** to life. Your power lies not in trying to bend life to your will, but in learning how to **flow** with it.

The Final Step: Trusting Yourself

The most important part of the Let Them Theory is **trusting yourself**. You have everything you need within you to create the life you want. You've been equipped with **inner wisdom**, the ability to make choices, and the strength to overcome obstacles. It's time to stop doubting your abilities and start believing that **you are enough**.

As you continue on your journey, remember that the process of letting go is ongoing. There will always be new layers to release, new patterns to shift, and new opportunities to embrace. But by mastering the principles of this theory, you'll build a foundation of **inner peace**, **confidence**, and **freedom** that will sustain you no matter what challenges lie ahead.

Final Thought: You Are Free

In the end, the Let Them Theory is not about achieving some final destination or completing a checklist of tasks. It's about **embracing freedom**—the freedom to live authentically, the freedom to trust the process, and the freedom to let go of everything that no longer serves you.

I leave you with these words from **Nelson Mandela**:

"I am not a saint, unless you think of a saint as a sinner who keeps on trying."

You may stumble. You may doubt. But as long as you keep trying, keep letting go, and keep trusting yourself, you will move closer to the life you deserve. A life filled with **peace**, **joy**, **purpose**, and **love**.

The ultimate freedom lies in letting go. Let it happen. Let it unfold. Trust that **you are exactly where you need to be**.

And with that, I wish you nothing but the best on this beautiful journey of **living life on your own terms**. Let go, and let life surprise you.

Thank You

Thank you for embarking on this journey with me. I hope the Let Them Theory has given you the tools, mindset, and courage to let go of the things that are holding you back and to embrace the life that is waiting for you. Keep practicing, keep growing, and remember: the power to create your best life is always in your hands.

The End.

Made in United States
Troutdale, OR
12/06/2024

26023144R10090